A GUIDE FOR MANAGERS OF HOME CARE SERVICES

Lesley Bell

D1465353

BOOKS

© 1996 Joint Initiative for Community Care Ltd
Published by Age Concern England
1268 London Road
London SW16 4ER

Editor Gillian Clarke
Design and production Eugenie Dodd Typographics
Copy preparation Vinnette Marshall
Printed in Great Britain by Bell & Bain Ltd, Glasgow

A catalogue record for this book is available from the British Library.

ISBN 0–86242–185–3

Contents

About the author 5

Acknowledgements 6

Introduction 7

1 The changing nature of home care 10

2 Managing the business 20

3 Managing service provision 37

4 Managing people 56

5 Managing the contract 76

6 Managing user-centred services 89

7 Managing yourself 99

Appendix 1 114
NVQ Management standards

Appendix 2 118
Example of manual handling risk assessment form

Appendix 3 124
Example of an accident record form

Appendix 4 128
Example of a job description

Appendix 5 130
Example of a person specification

Appendix 6 132
Sample interview questions: home care assistant

Appendix 7 134
Example of conditions of service

Appendix 8 136
Example of a disciplinary procedure

Appendix 9 138
Example of assessment of need form

Appendix 10 154
Example of a care plan

Further reading 159
Useful addresses 161
About Age Concern 163
Publications from ACE Books 164

Index 167

About the author

Since 1988, Lesley Bell has headed the work of the Joint Initiative for Community Care Limited. In 1991 JICC became a registered charity, owned jointly by the Association of Directors of Social Services and the Local Government Management Board.

Before setting up JICC, Lesley was a senior training adviser for 11 years in the Local Government Training Board, where she was responsible for developing training programmes and training material for social services staff, including home care assistants, home care managers and care assistants in homes for older people. She is Chair of the Joint Advisory Group of Domiciliary Care Associations and a non-executive director of the Bedford and Shires Community and Health Trust.

Lesley has done considerable work on the development of staff, managers and organisations throughout the personal social services. She has undertaken a number of activities in relation to community care, and was Project Manager for the development of the OPAL 2 package for care service managers on behalf of UNISON Education and Training. Lesley speaks regularly at seminars, conferences and workshops and is a frequent contributor to professional journals. She is also, of course, author of the very successful book for home care assistants, *CareFully*, published by Age Concern England.

Acknowledgements

My thanks are due to many people who helped to write this book. Particular thanks go to:

Berkshire County Council, for permission to use some of their material

Eileen Cooke

Linda How

Miranda Jones, The Homecare Partnership

Kent County Council, for statistics

Brenda McKie, St Helens Metropolitan Borough Council

Peter Smallridge, Chairman, Joint Initiative for Community Care Ltd (JICC)

Mary Thomas, Warwickshire County Council

Maggie Uttley, Director, British Association of Domiciliary Care Officers (BADCO)

and all those involved with home care whom I have met over the past 20 years and who, directly and indirectly, have contributed to the content of this book.

Lesley Bell
February 1996

Introduction

Managing the provision of care services can be one of the most reward-ing, absorbing and at the same time frustrating occupations! It attracts dedicated people who take up the work for a number of different reasons – some by chance, others because of related experience and knowledge such as nursing. Whatever their original reason for becoming a manager of home care services, most soon become committed and concerned to provide the highest possible quality of service to the people needing care.

Home care has come a long way since its origins as a service that gave help and support to mothers with children and babies. The present home care service has evolved from the Beveridge Report and the 1948 National Health and National Assistance Acts, which placed responsibility on local authorities to provide a home help service. However, the first recorded service was in 1897, the Jewish Sickroom Society. Then between 1918 and the 1930s cities such as Liverpool, Glasgow and Birmingham set up their own services.

Today assistance is provided not only to mothers and their families but also to people with physical disabilities, with learning disabilities or with mental health problems, living in their own homes within the community. However, approximately 85 per cent of home care is provided to older people who, for reasons of frailty, disability or illness, need some kind of support to enable them to continue to live in their own home.

Home care is *the* vital service that enables people to continue to live in their own home; enables them to live as independently as possible, within the limits of their own physical and mental capacity; and helps to keep families together when otherwise, owing to particular circumstances, they might be separated.

Originally, home care assistants, known then as home helps, provided a cleaning and shopping service, undertaking mainly the practical, physical tasks, managed and supervised by people known as home help organisers. Throughout the 1980s and 1990s, for reasons that will be explored in the next section, this emphasis changed. Home care now involves a wide range of personal care tasks, such as helping people to get up, take a bath and get dressed, as well as undertaking the more practical, physical tasks. In some cases home care provides the kind of assistance that might normally be expected of a nursing auxiliary or aide such as changing dressings, changing catheters and administering medicines. A rule of thumb is that home care does not generally involve tasks that 'intrude' into the body.

As a manager of home care services, you will be only too aware exactly how the task has changed and how complex it has become. Yet the original image of the home help, undertaking basic cleaning tasks, has proved extremely difficult to shift in the minds of most people not directly involved with the service. It is an image that must be dispelled if home care is to take its rightful place as providing the foundation on which other community services build. Without home care services, many older people would simply not be able to continue to live independently in their own homes. They would have to enter a residential or nursing home, or be cared for by a family carer until they too could no longer continue to cope with the strain.

One of the dilemmas with home care is that it increasingly involves more personal tasks and is being aimed particularly towards people with complex needs; however, many people, particularly those who have their own family carer, need only a cleaning service and not personal care. A 'cleaning only' service is now rarely available through local authority social services departments, unless it is part of a larger, more personal package of care, but other agencies, such as Age Concern through its local groups, have stepped in to provide basic cleaning services and to 'plug' the gap.

If home care is a vital service, it is effective management which ensures that the service is delivered to the people who need it, at the time and place that they need it and to the highest possible standard. Effective management enables services to be provided effectively and the users of the service to be satisfied with the care that they receive.

This book has been written to help you as a manager of home care services in the complex task you undertake. It is a sequel to *CareFully: A guide for home care assistants*, published by Age Concern England in 1993. Care has been taken to avoid repeating the content of that book but many of the threads, as they relate to the management task, are carried through into *Managing CareFully*.

There is inevitably a degree of overlap in the content of some of the chapters but I have tried to keep this to a minimum and refer you to other chapters as appropriate. Throughout the book there are checklists and summaries of Key Points, which I hope you will find useful. I have tried to avoid 'reinventing the wheel', so at times you will be referred to other documents that complement the content of *Managing CareFully*.

Each chapter, apart from the first, is related to levels 1 and 2 (NVQ 4 and 5) Management Standards. These are explained more fully in Chapter 7 and in Appendix 1 but completion of the activities in each chapter should provide evidence if you wish to obtain a full Management award. Chapter 1 provides underpinning knowledge and information, which is vital if you are to be an effective manager.

This book cannot be, nor is it intended to be, comprehensive. The specific task of manager will vary from organisation to organisation and there will undoubtedly be aspects of your particular role that are not included in this book. Nevertheless, I have made every effort to include the principal areas of activity required of managers of a home care service in the late 1990s.

I hope that you enjoy reading *Managing CareFully* and that it gives you plenty of ideas and food for thought.

1 The Changing Nature of Home Care

HOME CARE IN THE 1980s

The starting point must be the changes that have taken place in the provision of home care, beginning in the latter half of the 1980s and gathering momentum in the 1990s.

Throughout the 1970s and 80s the service was provided almost entirely by the local authority social services department to people who were referred to the department by someone such as their GP, family or friends and then assessed as needing home care.

Most authorities initially provided a free service but gradually, as demand increased and resources became relatively more limited, particularly in the 1980s, charges for the service were introduced by most local authorities. Sometimes this was a flat-rate charge, sometimes graduated depending upon the amount and level of care provided. People on Social Security or Income Support could, in the vast majority of cases, continue to receive a free service. A few authorities still provide a free home care service for all because charges for non-residential services are at the discretion of the local authority. However, as indicated in the *AMA Commentary* of 1994 and the 1995 *Survey of Changes for Social Care* from the Local Government Anti-Poverty Unit, government finance for local authorities is calculated on the basis of a supposed 9 per cent collected income, which in practice forces most departments to make some kind of charge for the service.

Throughout the 1980s the service evolved from home help to home care – incorporating personal care tasks with more practical care. New forms of home care service emerged such as night sitting, care in the period immediately after discharge from hospital and help with getting up and going to bed.

Why did this happen? There are two main reasons. The first is that demographic change was beginning to make an impact, more people living longer resulting in a corresponding increase in care needs. This increase in demand was contained to a considerable extent by the increased number of places in privately run residential homes, the cost of which was met from the Social Security budget for people unable to meet the cost themselves.

NUMBER OF OLDER PEOPLE IN THE UK

	aged 65+ (millions)	aged 80+ (millions)
1971	7.38	1.29
1981	8.46	1.58
1991	9.07	2.14
2001*	9.39	2.57

*estimated figures   Source: *Social Trends* (1995)

RESIDENTIAL AND NURSING HOME PLACES IN THE UK (ALL SECTORS)

	1980	1988	1993
Residential homes (adults)	214,500	304,400	313,100
Nursing homes	27,200	78,300	166,500

Source: Laing's *Review of Private Healthcare* (1995)

However, growing numbers of older and very much older people also increased the volume and nature of demand for home care. This led to home care services taking on new tasks and responsibilities as well as extending existing ones. At the same time, Government was introducing both financial limits on spending by local authorities and penalties for exceeding these limits (a surcharge known as 'capping'). This led many authorities to introduce a charge for the provision of home care.

A series of inspections of eight local authority county council home care services was undertaken by the Social Services Inspectorate of the Department of Health between 1985 and 1988. As a result, it was generally recommended in those departments which were inspected that home care services be provided primarily to people with intensive or complex care needs rather than to those who required only practical care (eg cleaning and shopping).

THE IMPACT OF COMMUNITY CARE POLICIES

Sir Roy Griffiths' report, *Community Care – An Agenda for Action*, published in 1988, proved to be a turning point for home care. It placed priority on the care of people in their own homes as opposed to the care of people in residential homes. This complemented the policy, already operating within the National Health Service (NHS), of closing long-stay hospital wards and institutions for older people and people with learning disabilities or with mental health problems, and supporting them in the community.

Responsibility for community care was to be given to local authority social services departments, a recommendation endorsed in 1989 in the Government's response to the Griffiths' report – the White Paper *Caring for People – Community Care in the Next Decade and Beyond*. This made the development of domiciliary care the first of Government's six key objectives:

1 To promote the development of domiciliary, day and respite services to enable people to live in their own homes wherever feasible and sensible.

2 To ensure that service providers make practical support for carers a high priority.

3 To make proper assessment of need and good care management the cornerstone of high quality care.

4 To promote the development of a flourishing independent sector alongside good quality public services.

5 To clarify the responsibilities of agencies and so make it easier to hold them to account for their performance.

6 To secure better value for taxpayers' money by introducing a new funding structure for social care.

From *Caring for People*: paragraph 1.11.

These key objectives introduced a number of other concepts that have had an impact on the home care service in the 1990s. They have become the underpinning values or principles of community care:

- The promotion of the independent sector in the provision of care services, resulting in the significant growth in the number of private sector agencies and voluntary organisations (including Age Concern) providing home care.

- Focusing on assessing the real needs of the person rather than on the services available (ie 'needs' or 'user' led rather than service led).

- Separating the assessment of needs, and the development of 'packages' of care to meet those needs, from the actual provision of care services. This is commonly referred to as the 'purchaser/provider split'.

- Local authority social services departments becoming primarily 'enabling' agencies, contracting for services and making the maximum possible use of private and voluntary sector providers.

- Developing a range of services that provide the widest possible range of options for people receiving care and thus maximise their choice.

- Maintaining and improving standards and providing quality services.

Under the NHS and Community Care Act 1990, responsibility for community care was transferred to local authority social services departments from April 1993. From April 1992, all local authorities were required to consult widely and then publish an annual Community Care Plan identifying the care needs of the local community and the ways in which the authority proposed to meet those needs.

Implementation of the new community care policies was funded by the transfer of money (the Special Transitional Grant or STG) from the Social Security budget (which had paid for the care of people in residential homes) to local authorities. The money transferred was 'ring-fenced' – it could be spent only on community care. In England (but not in Wales, Scotland or Northern Ireland) 85 per cent of the transferred money has to be spent in the purchase of services from the independent sector: private or voluntary sector agencies or NHS Trusts (which are considered by Government to be part of the independent sector).

It is easy to assume that the changes which have taken place in the nature and provision of home care in the 1990s are the direct result of the implementation of the NHS and Community Care Act. However, it is worth recognising that, even if the Act had never been introduced, many of the changes (eg the stimulation of the private and voluntary sectors, local authorities becoming 'enabler' rather than primary providers and the development of 'user-centred' services) would have happened anyway as part of the shift in thinking about the management and provision of public sector services. These changes had already had a major impact on public sector housing, education and the NHS.

The significant difference that the Act made was that, by making local authorities responsible for assessing the need for care (including residential care) and providing them with money to do it (the STG), Government was able to put an end to the spiralling costs of supporting people in residential care through the Social Security budget, some £2,500 million in 1992/93 from a base figure of approximately £10 million in 1979/80.

Since April 1993 the cost of providing care for anyone unable to meet the whole cost themselves, either in their own home or in a residential home, has been met from the limited budgets of the social services departments. The previously unlimited funding of residential care through the Social Security budget is no longer available.

Towards the end of the second year of funding community care, many local authorities found that they were heading for a significant over-spend on the community care budget. There were three principal reasons for this:

- Changes in the way in which the STG was allocated in the second year, which meant that some authorities received less funding than they had anticipated.

- A considerable increase in the demand for care and in the number of people coming forward to have their needs assessed (650,000 people in England and Wales in 1994/95 in contrast to 500,00 the previous year).

- People living longer when provided with care in their own homes than had been expected.

In addition, some people who had previously arranged and paid for their own care realised that it could be provided at less cost to themselves by having their needs assessed by the local social services department. The situation was made more difficult by a reduction in the amount of money given by central government in 1995/96 to local government (known as the Revenue Support Grant).

The limited funding available for community care has meant that local authorities have had to introduce levels of priority in terms of need and increasingly tighter eligibility criteria in order to ensure that the people most in need receive the care services they require.

At the same time, radical changes have taken place in the health service. The closure of long-stay hospital and geriatric wards, new surgical techniques and advances in medicine are all factors contributing to the earlier discharge of patients from hospital. The continual pressure to obtain 'value for money' and to reduce waiting lists has also resulted in patients being discharged from hospital back into the community at the earliest possible opportunity.

The emphasis on developing user-centred services focusing on the specific needs of the person receiving care is resulting in an end to the restrictive 9–5, Monday to Friday, service and the emergence of 24-hour care seven days a week. The inevitable outcome is an increase in the volume and complexity of the work of the home care service and a gradual withdrawal of local authority funding for purely practical, physical care except in special circumstances such as the support of a family carer. Although this shift away from providing a significant volume of practical care has not yet happened in many authorities, it almost certainly will eventually.

Who now provides home care?

Home care services are now provided by:

- Local authority social service departments – the 'in-house' provision.
- Voluntary organisations such as Crossroads and the Leonard Cheshire Foundation which have provided home care services for many years.
- Voluntary organisations entering into the provision of home care for the first time (eg Age Concern).
- Private agencies run for profit.
- Private agencies run on a not-for-profit basis and co-operatives.
- Private agencies that are part of a franchise operation.
- Nursing agencies extending into the provision of home care.
- Residential homes diversifying into home care.

■ NHS trusts extending their community nursing services to include personal care.

As the provision of intensive home care services increases, the differences in roles and responsibilities between the health service (district nurses) and social services (home care) become increasingly blurred. The example often quoted is that of helping someone take a bath – if the help is provided by nursing staff, it is a 'health' bath; if by a home care assistant, it is a 'social' bath. Other examples include the administration of medicines, and changing catheters and dressings.

Whilst the provision of in-house services is decreasing, the provision of home care services by all the other organisations is increasing. As a manager of home care services, you may be working in any one of them. Although there are differences between various providers, the fundamental task of managing home care services is, or should be, very similar.

Purchasers of home care

By far the most significant purchaser of home care is the local authority. The total net expenditure in England and Wales is estimated to have been £536,546,000 in 1993/94 (source: the Chartered Institute of Public Finance and Accountability) an increasing amount of which is spent in the private and voluntary sectors.

Most social services departments have staff whose particular responsibility is the assessment of care needs and developing packages of care to meet those needs. These 'care managers' then 'purchase' the services from either the in-house provider or a provider in the private or voluntary sector – generally by placing 'spot' contracts, sometimes by commissioning the service from an established, larger, 'block' contract. This process is known as care management. For further information, see Chapter 5 of this book, the *Community Care Handbook* and the OPAL package listed in the Further Reading.

Although as a manager of home care you will not normally be involved in care management, you do need to understand the process that leads to the commissioning and provision of your services. Your staff should be familiar with the content of the care plan for each person they care for and be aware of the desired outcomes from the service they are providing (this is covered in *CareFully*, chapter 1).

It is not unknown for home care managers to undertake their own assessment of need when being allocated a new person to receive the service, rather than accept the assessment of the care manager. Whilst this is understandable, it should not be necessary in practice. If it *is* necessary, it indicates either a lack of ability in assessment on the part of the person undertaking the care management function or a lack of trust on the part of the home care service manager. Ideally, you should be able to work with your purchasers to provide the most effective service possible.

The Health and Safety at Work Act 1974 requires that a risk assessment be undertaken. This *can* be done by care managers when care needs are assessed and the package to meet those needs is developed. The assessment of the risks involved in delivering the care package should be part of the commissioning and contracting function. In practice, this does not often happen because the people involved in the purchase of services from provider organisations have rarely had the training or possess the skills to undertake an accurate risk assessment. It is thus often left to the home care manager to identify any health and safety risks associated with the provision of care to a particular person.

If you manage a local authority in-house home care service, you may also undertake some assessment of need in simple, straightforward cases where the need for home care (as opposed to any other service) seems self-evident. However, this is contrary to the 'needs-led' rather than 'service-led' approach introduced with community care, because the assessment of need is no longer independent of the service provided to meet that need.

In complex situations and assessments for multiple services, the lead in the care management process may be taken by a professional from another organisation: for example, a district nurse or physiotherapist from a health authority or trust who will purchase the care services on behalf of the local authority social services department.

There is of course a large market for home care in the private sector:

- people with care needs and their families who are not eligible for services from the local authority;
- people who choose not to seek local authority assistance and are able to meet the cost of the care themselves.

This is likely to be an expanding market in the future, particularly if the demand for insurance policies to pay for community care increases.

Conflicts in the system

There are a number of conflicts and contradictions in the system, of which you, as a manager of services, are no doubt aware. The most obvious ones to note here are:

- The pressure to reduce costs and obtain value for money while setting high standards and delivering high quality services – quality always has a cost attached.

- The need to provide services to the people with the greatest need, using strict eligibility criteria while also providing help and support to family carers.

- Health services are generally provided free of charge but a charge is levied for the provision of home care in all but a very few local authorities.

- Until very recently, VAT at the standard rate has been levied on care provided to people living in their own home but not if they were living in a residential care home. From 1 January 1996, home care is exempt from VAT provided the service is managed by qualified medical or nursing staff.

- Under the Registered Homes Act 1984, private and voluntary sector residential homes have to be registered with the local authority Registration and Inspection Unit; all homes, including the local authority's own homes, must be inspected at least twice a year to ensure that they meet the required standards. There is at present no similar requirement to register, regulate and inspect agencies providing care to people in their own homes.

Can you identify any other contradictions that are significant for you in managing your business?

KEY POINTS

- Social services departments fund the provision of all community care, including residential care, following an assessment of the care needs.

- An increasing number of people with complex care needs are cared for in their own homes who would previously have entered residential or nursing homes.

- The distinction between health care and social care for people in their own home is becoming increasingly blurred.

- Levels of priority for services and increasingly stringent criteria for eligibility have been introduced.

- Assessment of care needs is now separated from the provision of services in many social services departments.

- Social services departments purchase home care from private and voluntary agencies as well from their own in-house providers.

- In England (but not Wales, Scotland or Northern Ireland) 85 per cent of the additional money provided for community care *must* be spent in the independent sector.

- As a result, there has been a significant rise in the number of private sector agencies providing home care.

- Voluntary organisations are becoming providers of home care. Health Trusts are considered to be part of the independent sector, and some are beginning to provide intensive home care services.

- Competition is therefore increased.

- Expansion of in-house services is limited and in some places they have been cut back.

- The emphasis is on high quality, user-centred services.

- Business practices must be applied to the purchase and provision of home care.

2 Managing the Business

This chapter relates to the following Management standards:

M1 1.1, 2.1, 2.2, 3.1, 3.2, 8.1, 8.2

M2 1.1, 1.2, 2.1, 3.1, 3.2, 4.1, 4.2, 9.1–9.3

BUSINESS PLANNING – WHY PLAN?

Whether you manage a local authority home care service, a private sector home care agency or a voluntary organisation involved in the provision of home care, it is essential to plan the development of the service or business, both in the short term and in the longer term.

Why?

The first reason is that it is good practice to plan effectively and to be proactive – anticipating what is, or may be, going to happen before it actually does – rather than reactive – responding after the event, usually placing you and your service at a disadvantage. Business planning therefore gives you an advantage by enabling you to plan ahead and respond to changing demands. Obviously there will always be unforeseen circumstances and events, but planning the business helps you to reduce these to a minimum.

Secondly, business planning – for the service as a whole or just for your part of it – enables you to identify exactly what you (and others) should be doing. It helps to clarify roles and who should be doing what. It also identifies any gaps in the way in which you manage and provide the service.

It is essential to set clear aims and objectives. Others, including people receiving your services and those commissioning them, need to know what the overall aim or purpose of your organisation is and its specific objectives. These of course should be consistent with the underpinning values or principles identified in Chapter 3.

Business planning takes the aims and objectives a step further, to enable you to identify financial and performance targets and to set timescales. These in turn enable you to measure the progress of your agency or team and to monitor your performance.

It is easy to be ambitious in setting targets and timescales, particularly if you are enthusiastic about the business. But do try to be realistic. Admirable though it may be to set ambitious targets, it becomes dispiriting and demoralising if you fail to achieve them – I speak here from hard experience!

If yours is a voluntary or private sector organisation seeking financial support and investment from a bank or other financial institution, you will almost certainly be required to prepare a detailed business plan. This will be used to assess the risk involved and to decide the amount that will actually be lent in both the short and the longer term.

Considerable mystique has been built up around business planning and of course to a certain extent it is 'flavour of the month' or even decade! It has been introduced along with other aspects of providing public services on a more business-like basis such as the stimulation of the mixed economy, the separation of the commissioning from the provision of services and thus the introduction of contracts and competition.

However, in the final analysis, business planning is simply good practice, which can be summarised as:

- To be proactive
- To give your business an advantage over others
- To reduce unforeseen circumstances to a minimum
- To clarify roles and who should be doing what
- To identify gaps in your service

- To inform those receiving and/or purchasing your services
- To set clear aims, objectives and targets
- To obtain financial backing from banks and other institutions

What does a business plan look like?

Business plans come in all shapes and sizes, and there is no single way to develop one. The two key tests of an effective business plan are:

- Does it tell you and your colleagues all you need to know to manage and develop your business or organisation effectively?
- Does it tell others outside the organisation all they need to know? (This includes organisations purchasing your care services on behalf of others – ie the local authority social services department, the people receiving your care and the financial institutions investing in your organisation.)

You can obtain a proforma for business planning from any high street bank. These are, of course, very general, intended for any type of business, but they will give you a good start and indicate exactly the kind of information the bank is seeking. Most banks have a small business adviser who can assist you and provide advice.

Another proforma, developed specifically for planning a home care business, may be found in the *Standards for Registration for Domiciliary Care*, produced by the Joint Advisory Group of Domiciliary Care Associations. *Home Care: The business of caring*, published by Age Concern England, contains a checklist of key questions on what should go into a business plan. (See Further Reading.)

So what should your business plan cover? The following checklist may help. Much of what should be incorporated into your business plan is covered in the following chapters in this book.

It may seem a formidable and time-consuming undertaking to produce a business plan. Once you have completed it for the first time, though, subsequent business plans build upon the first so there is no need to start from scratch each time.

Contents of the business plan

Factual information about the organisation

Name of organisation

Address of main office

Telephone/fax numbers

Address of registered office (if different)

Address(es) of branch office(s) if any

Date organisation was established or incorporated

Nature of the business; geographical area covered

Name of owner or parent company

Names of main board directors

Resources available, including capital and equipment

References

Name and address of bank

Name and address of accountants

Name and address of auditors

Financial information

Turnover:

> last two or three years

> current year (projected)

> next year (target)

Turnover broken down by factors such as services provided, geographical area, etc.

Costs of running the business, broken down by main cost areas

Creditors and debtors analysis

Profit and loss forecast

Value of contracts from local authorities and other purchasers

Level of insurance carried

Structure of organisation (or section, unit)

Organisation chart

Name of most senior manager responsible, and qualifications

Details of other managers, and their qualifications

Details of care staff, full and part time, and any qualifications held

Ratio of manager:care staff:users of the service

Range of services provided

Include some indication of weighting: which services you provide most often and which the least often

Market analysis

Total size

Percentage share of the market (estimated)

Main competitors: their strengths and weaknesses

Pricing structure

Purchasers: local authority, private/voluntary sectors

Information on people receiving the service

Number of people receiving care now and 12 months earlier

Projection for the next 12 months

Number of hours of care provided

People receiving care by categories of need (eg frail older people, chronically sick people, mentally infirm older people, mothers and children, people with learning disabilities, people with physical disabilities, people with mental health problems)

Business in current financial year

Aims

Objectives

Targets

Known business

Projected business

New possibilities for development

Longer term projections

Business in previous financial year

A comparison between the actual and the projected

You may wish to compile a comprehensive detailed business plan for use within your organisation and make a summary to share with other organisations and people.

The Community Care Plan

Don't forget the Community Care Plan. Every local authority social services department must publish a plan every year. It is a public document and you should obtain a copy from your local authority. If you work in more than one authority, make sure you obtain the plans for each one because they will be different.

The Community Care Plan is a good source of information for your business plan. It provides extremely useful data on demographic trends in the authority and on the purchasing intentions of the social services department. The plan will also provide you with information on future care needs and the department's priorities over the next three to five years.

It may also identify priorities and eligibility criteria for the provision of services. If these are not in the Community Care Plan, obtain the relevant documents that do contain the information: it must be published and made generally available. This is important because it tells you:

■ The type of service the authority will be purchasing on behalf of people needing care.

■ The services that the department will not be purchasing or providing itself (ie a potential market for others).

The local authority must consult widely with all sectors when developing the Community Care Plan. You may wish to make sure that you or your organisation is included in the consultation process. Contact your local social services department for further information.

Monitoring the business plan

Why should you monitor the implementation and effectiveness of your business plan? Well, if your business plan is effective, it should provide the framework within which you operate your business. By monitoring progress on the implementation of the plan, you are, in effect, monitoring the progress of your business.

Another reason for monitoring the plan is that it should highlight any potential areas of difficulty (eg cashflow problems) and enable you to take appropriate action before the situation becomes too serious. Monitoring the plan will also enable you to be prepared for any emergencies that may occur.

Failure to monitor the plan effectively may risk your relationship and credibility with the bank and with your staff. Ultimately, it may adversely affect the service you provide to the people needing care.

Expanding the service

The business plan should identify any opportunities for expansion in either the short or the longer term. Organisations providing home care are generally very cautious about expansion because it can place a considerable strain on all involved, both managers and staff, stretch limited resources to the breaking point and put a strain on cashflow.

If the social services department is your principal client and you have expanded to meet their needs in the short term, you may find it difficult to recruit the right calibre of staff in the time available. You could also have difficulty financially if the placing of (spot) contracts slows down and some of the people you are caring for no longer require your services or die. Placing too much reliance on spot contracts is dangerous because they are, by their very nature, unpredictable. If at all possible, it is preferable to obtain a form of block contract that enables you to plan the future of the business more effectively (see Chapter 5).

Whenever you consider expanding the business, always consult both your accountant and your bank who will give you practical advice and assistance that will enable you to expand in a planned and systematic way. They will also advise you of any risks if you wish to expand quickly. The saying is: 'Taxi on the runway for a while before taking off!'

FINANCE AND ADMINISTRATION

An essential part of running and planning a business is keeping up to date with the finance and administration. It is all too easy to let it slip – but you can't afford to.

The key to successful financial management is an appropriate financial management software program for the computer such as Sage. Although it may take you time to learn how to use it, it will save you time and effort in the long run.

Unit costs

It is essential to know your unit costs. That means what it costs you as a unit or organisation to provide one hour of care. Without knowing what your actual unit costs are, you cannot work out accurately the cost of providing your service. If you are not aware of your unit costs you are likely to consistently under-charge, which in a very short time will lead you into financial difficulties because expenditure consistently exceeds income.

On the other hand, you may over-charge, which will lose you business unless you are providing a specialised or 'market niche' service.

Knowing your *true* unit costs enables you to make informed decisions about what to charge the people and organisations purchasing, or considering purchasing, your services. It also helps if you know the unit costs of your competitors – but that information is often harder to obtain!

Unit costs vary considerably. For example, the more complex care you provide, the more you will pay staff for specialist or professional skills, which in turn will increase your unit costs. Similarly, the more you have to pay for your office accommodation, the greater will be your unit costs.

Keeping the overheads as low as possible is an important way of controlling the unit costs. Overheads are those elements that contribute to the total cost of running the unit or organisation but are not directly attributable to the cost of providing the care.

The cost of providing one hour of care includes:

- Pay of home carer plus 'on costs' (employer's contribution, including national insurance, pension and overheads, annual leave, sick pay)
- Travel expenses for the home carer, including the time taken
- Pay of management plus 'on costs'
- Pay of administrative and clerical staff, plus 'on costs'
- Running costs of central office – including hire of equipment, telephone, business rates, water, gas, electricity, etc
- Other overheads, including insurance, cost of financial loans, marketing, advertising and promotional activities, staff training, etc

All divided by the number of hours of care provided.

NOTE There may be costs in addition to the unit costs. For example, the cost of collecting the financial contribution of the person receiving care.

The unit costs of private and voluntary agencies are invariably lower than those of local authority in-house services. However hard in-house services try to reduce their costs to a minimum, they can rarely reduce the overheads to a level comparable to that of most of the providers in the independent sector. This is because of the need to pay a contribution to the running of the corporate centre of the local authority and because most local authorities are still tied into national conditions of service and pay. Some authorities do not include these costs in their calculation of unit costs; others have sought to overcome the problem by placing their home care service at 'arm's length' from the authority and therefore semi-autonomous.

The relatively high unit cost of providing 'in-house' home care places this service at a considerable disadvantage when in competition with agencies and organisations in the private and voluntary sectors. It is therefore only a matter of time before some local authorities consider transferring the home care service into the independent sector as 'trusts', as a number have already done with residential homes.

Large home care agencies in the private and voluntary sectors will also have to watch that, as they expand, the overheads do not creep up because of the cost of running a large bureaucratic centre.

Monitoring the cashflow

Monitoring the cashflow (ie the money coming in and going out of the organisation) is essential if the organisation is to remain commercially viable and competitive. Regular monitoring enables you to keep track of your debtors, which is particularly important if you have contracts with local authorities as they are notoriously slow payers. However, many authorities have now speeded up payments in recognition that delay can cause difficulties with the organisations that are contracted to provide services on their behalf.

If you do experience delays in being paid for your services, over and above the standard 30 days, it is always worth talking to the authority or organisation to see if anything can be done to speed up payment. It is not, after all, in their interest to cause you cashflow problems, as that will result in your providing a lower quality service on their behalf; if, ultimately, the delay puts the business in jeopardy, it will cost the authority a considerable sum of money to find and contract with a new supplier.

One of the ways to speed up payment is the BACS system (Bank Automated Credit System) which enables debtors to transfer payment directly into your bank account. The disadvantage of this is that it can be difficult to keep track of payments unless you are informed when they are made. The BACS system could also be used to pay staff wages because it is simpler and more efficient.

Most small businesses monitor the cashflow on a weekly and a monthly basis. You should always arrange for your bank to send you regular statements – at least monthly, so that you can keep track of your financial position.

At the beginning of this main section I said that you should invest in a good financial software system. With this you can computerise your accounts, invoicing and payroll. Most of the systems currently available enable you to adapt the software to meet the particular needs of your organisation and unit. Even if you are a small agency, you will soon find such systems invaluable.

Systems that provide financial information for in-house providers of home care are also invaluable in monitoring and keeping track of the budget. This will give you early warning of any projected over-spend and you can take the necessary corrective action. Many in-house providers are now operating on the basis of a block contract with the purchasers of care in their own department. They have to keep track of income and expenditure in a similar way to voluntary and private sector agencies.

Remember that, with anything to do with finance, it is always important to develop and maintain a close working relationship with your accountant and with your bank in order to create confidence in your business and support when you need it most.

Administration

It is easy to overlook administration as a small or not very important part of the management task. However, it is a vital cog in the 'wheel' of a home care organisation! You forget about administration at your peril.

What do we mean by administration? Basically it is about putting the systems in place and using them appropriately so that the organisation can operate effectively. Monitoring income and expenditure and using financial management software systems (discussed in the previous section) are all part of financial administration, but you will also have to ensure that you have other records and systems in place. You need record systems for (for example):

- your customers – the people receiving care from your organisation
- your purchasers, when they are different from your customers
- staff employment and training
- complaints and compliments
- accidents

As with financial records, most of these records are stored most efficiently and effectively on a computerised system, with software packages purchased 'off-the-shelf' and adapted to the needs of your organisation.

Under the Health and Safety at Work Act 1974, all accidents must be reported on an accident report form and entered into an accident record book. (See the section later in this chapter, on legal requirements, and Appendix 3 for an example of an accident record form.) If you provide services on behalf of the local authority and/or are part of a local authority voluntary registration scheme or 'approved provider' list, you will also be required to report serious accidents to the local authority, usually within seven days.

Local authority in-house providers are required to record all complaints and to take appropriate action promptly. It is good practice for voluntary and private sector agencies also to record complaints – many local authority specifications for tenders require such a system to be in place. However, it is also good practice and a morale boost for staff to record the compliments that are received as well as the complaints. This helps to put the complaints into perspective and supports positive public relations.

The accurate recording of complaints is a valuable management tool because it provides you with feedback on the quality of service provided. It will also give you warning of any problems that may be developing and so enable you to take the necessary corrective action before they become too severe.

Any of these systems and records, whether computerised or not, must comply with the requirements of the Data Protection Act 1984 and the Personal Protection Act 1989 and be kept in a place where confidentiality can be maintained. (See the section later in this chapter on legal requirements.)

NOTE Do not keep confidential client records on a computer screen where anyone walking into the room can read them. It does happen!

Insurance

Providing care to people in their own homes is a high-risk area, for a number of different reasons, so it is extremely important that organisations and agencies have adequate insurance cover. Individual care staff will need to be covered as well as the agency itself or the employing organisation.

The reason why the risks in home care are higher than in other work is that the employing organisation has little, if any, control over the work environment. It is well known that the majority of accidents occur in the home. There will therefore be naturally occurring hazards that are either not anticipated or not present when the assessment of the risks was undertaken. In addition, care staff are working on their own, unsupervised, and may risk doing things that they might otherwise not do.

Local authority home care staff should be covered by the local authority personal accident insurance. All other organisations and agencies in the voluntary and private sectors will also need to take out cover – both professional liability insurance and indemnity insurance. The amount of cover required by local authorities, when contracting with the private and voluntary sectors to provide home care on behalf of the authority, varies between £1 million and £5 million, the majority requiring £3 million.

There are companies that specialise in insurance cover for home care. The United Kingdom Home Care Association (UKHCA) has negotiated special rates for its members. However, it is always worth going to an insurance broker. They are in a position to 'shop around' and it will save you time and effort.

If you don't already have a policy and therefore no established track record in a related area of work (eg residential care), the premiums may be as high as £1,500–£2,000 per year. This will be reviewed annually and reduced if you make no claims.

Ironically, one of the reasons why the premiums are so high is that there is no regulation of the agencies and organisations providing home care. From the point of view of the insurance companies this increases the risk factor, and therefore the premiums.

You will need to be very careful when you write your policies and procedures, to be sure that you are covered for all eventualities. Otherwise, exclusions must be specifically written into your policies. For example, home care staff frequently help the people they are caring for with their medication. Be sure that you are covered for this, in case anything goes wrong. If you do not have cover, instruct staff accordingly.

Care staff who are registered self-employed have a responsibility to take out their own personal accident and third party liability insurance. If you manage an agency that recruits self-employed care staff, you should always check that they have adequate insurance cover. It is also worth while, if possible, ensuring that the people receiving the care have personal accident insurance.

More than 50 per cent of claims on an employer's liability insurance are made by staff for injury sustained while at work. This type of injury is mainly the result of lack of training in safe working practices or proper induction, so make sure that staff are properly trained.

Because of the increasing number of fraudulent claims being made, insurance companies are becoming more rigorous in investigating claims. They will be looking closely at your policies and procedures to ensure that you have taken precautions against accidents.

LEGAL REQUIREMENTS

It is important to keep abreast of relevant legislation – a difficult task that is complicated by the issue of EC Regulations which affect different aspects of providing a home care service.

The main laws with which you should comply are listed below. However, they are by no means the only legislation that applies. The licence to practise required under the Nurses Agency Act applies only if you are providing professionally qualified nursing staff – it does not apply to care staff in general.

Significant legislation

Nurses Agency Act 1957

Health and Safety at Work Act 1974

Sex Discrimination Act 1976

Race Relations Act 1976

Data Protection Act 1984

Companies Act 1985

Control of Substances Harmful to Health Act (COSHH) 1988

Personal Protection Act 1989

Manual Lifting and Handling EC Regulations 1993

Carers (Recognition and Services) Act 1995

You will note that there is no legislation, relating to the provision of care to people in their own homes, equivalent to the Residential Homes Act

1984. At present home care is unregulated, apart from voluntary registration and accreditation schemes operated by a number of social services departments.

You can obtain information about employment legislation, PAYE, National Insurance and VAT regulations from your local branch of the Inland Revenue and HM Customs and Excise. Your own accountant will also be able to advise you, and even tell you what it all means in practice!

Contact the Office of the Data Protection Registrar for a very helpful information pack on the legislation (see the Useful Addresses section).

Information about the implications of the Health and Safety legislation may be obtained from your local branch of the Health and Safety Executive – look up the address in your *Yellow Pages*.

For information on other legislation (eg the Race Relations Act), visit your local reference library. The library is a major source of much useful information.

There are other laws that will apply; for example, that pertaining to disabled persons and EC law on the rights of part-time workers. The easiest way to keep abreast of the legislation is through the professional journals and the social work press. Members of the professional associations such as BADCO and UKHCA receive regular updates on the legislation through their Associations' bulletins.

This section mentions only the laws with which you must comply in order to run your business. There is of course other legislation with which you must be familiar which relates to the professional practice of managing and providing a home care service. This is covered in Chapter 3.

MARKETING AND PUBLICITY

These never stop! You need to ensure that your business is promoted positively at every opportunity. This includes:

- The image and appearance of your information and publicity material. Amateurish or scruffy leaflets will give the impression of an organisation that is not concerned about quality and is unlikely to adopt a professional approach to the management and provision of care.

- Your own personal image is also important as that too conveys a message about the organisation and the way in which it is managed. However, take care: it is possible to 'over-sell' as well as 'under-sell' yourself.

- The image and behaviour of your staff. They are your most valuable asset in promoting the image of the organisation, as they are in regular contact with people needing care. If staff feel valued and motivated and enjoy the work they are doing, they will convey an important message to others and be an excellent advertisement for the organisation. Remember that a considerable volume of new business is generated by word of mouth.

Where should you advertise?

A list of places to advertise is given below. Sometimes this means placing an advertisement; at other times it means leaving leaflets. Promote the services you provide through:

- GP surgeries
- Carers' groups
- *Yellow Pages*
- Shop windows
- Day centres
- Local library
- Local free newspaper

Consider the cost of not appearing in local directories: this is very often the first place that people purchasing care, and their family carer, will turn to for the names and addresses of organisations able to provide care.

Although there is no statutory regulation of home care agencies nationally, an increasing number of social services departments are introducing voluntary schemes or lists of approved providers. You should find out if your local authority has such a scheme and, if so, how you get on to the 'approved' list. Most authorities with such schemes will only contract for the provision of care with agencies that are on the list. Moreover, social services departments are a useful source of referral for people who are seeking private home care and are able to pay for themselves.

Further information on marketing and publicity

I can only touch on marketing and publicity in this book, but there are a number of sources you can go to for further information. For example:

- OPAL 2 Module 2 distance learning material for managers of care services, which contains a complete unit on marketing and market research (see Further Reading).
- Banks provide starter packs that include information on marketing.
- Local Enterprise Agencies/TECs run free and subsidised courses on business administration, including marketing.
- Finally, see section 5 of *Home Care: The business of caring*, published by Age Concern England, for further ideas (see Further Reading).

KEY POINTS

- Planning your business helps you to identify potential problems in advance and reduces the likelihood of unforeseen circumstances arising.
- Business planning helps you to monitor the performance of your agency or organisation.
- The business plan in successive years should build on the previous year's plan.
- Use the information in the annual Community Care Plan produced by your local authority to 'inform' your business plan.
- Work out in detail the unit costs of providing your service.
- Monitor your cashflow and find ways, such as the BACS system, of speeding up payment.
- Keep all your records systems up to date, preferably by obtaining a suitable computer software program.
- Make sure you keep abreast of and comply with the requirements of relevant legislation, including EC directives.
- Make sure that you market and promote your service effectively. Marketing never stops!

3 Managing Service Provision

This chapter relates to the following Management standards:

M1 1.1, 1.2, 6.1, 6.2
M2 1.5, 2.3, 2.4, 7.1, 7.2

POLICIES AND PROCEDURES

Managing the provision of care to people in their own home is a complex task. People who are not directly involved in home care assume that the management task is no different from that in any other care service. There are, though, a number of features that make home care significantly different.

■ Home care staff work in people's own homes, a work environment over which the manager has little, if any, control.

■ The vast majority of home care staff work on their own with the person they are caring for.

■ The work of home care staff is unsupervised on a daily or even weekly basis. The standard of the work may therefore go unchecked for a considerable time.

■ Unlike other people who work in comparable situations (eg district nurses), most home care staff have received only very limited training and do not hold a professional qualification.

■ An increasing volume of care is being provided at unsocial hours – early morning, late evening and at weekends – which makes supervision even more difficult.

Most home care staff work on their own but they should not work in a vacuum. One way in which you as a manager can help in reducing the isolation is to ensure that the organisation, agency or unit in which you work has in place a set of policies, practices and procedures. These should provide the framework within which you and the home care staff work.

These policies and procedures should be compiled in consultation with the care staff and anyone else who will be responsible for their implementation. This will ensure that they are based on the practical experiences of staff and extend ownership. Once agreed, all staff should have copies of the policies and procedures that relate to their area of work (see also Chapter 4). It will also be appropriate to include most, if not all, the policies in the information provided for people receiving care.

Most people groan at the thought of introducing policies and procedures because they associate it with bureaucracy and unnecessary paperwork. But a policy need not be a long document – in fact, the shorter the better because staff are more likely to read it and remember it. One paragraph, or even one sentence, may suffice.

The rest of this chapter explores key areas in which you need to develop policies and procedures. Subsequent chapters consider putting them into practice.

AIMS AND OBJECTIVES

You need to set clear aims and objectives for the service you provide so that staff, purchasers of care services, people receiving care and people investing in your organisation are all clear about the nature of the business. You may recall that Chapter 2 included the aims and objectives of the organisation in the business plan.

The aim should be a broad statement, which may be modified over time but will generally apply for a number of years. For example:

- To provide a flexible, personal and practical care service to people living in their own homes or living with relatives or friends.

Objectives are more specific and may change more frequently as different market opportunities open up. Your organisation may have several objectives at any one time. For example:

- To provide care services to older people and adults with disabilities at a time that is most suited to their needs and circumstances.

- To provide a personal care service, combined with practical care as required.

- To provide 24-hour respite care in people's own homes.

Targets are identified annually in relation to each of the objectives, and form a key element in the business plan. For example:

1 To provide an average of 500 hours of care per week to 50 people.

2 To increase the number of hours of care provided by at least 10 per cent by the end of the financial year.

Both objectives and targets should be precise, realistic, achievable and measurable.

So the overall process is:

Identify ⟶ Clarify ⟶ Set annual
broad aims   objectives   targets

Aims, objectives and targets may be set for the organisation or agency as a whole and for sections or teams within it. If they are identified for a small part of a larger organisation, the aims and objectives of the section or team should be consistent with the overall aims of the whole organisation. Aims and objectives for teams should be less general, and more specific and focused, than the aims and objectives for the whole organisation.

Underpinning values

Having determined the aims, objectives and targets for the organisation, the next stage is to identify the values that should underpin the service. This issue was explored in the first chapter of *CareFully*. In the midst of the changes taking place in the provision of home care and the application of business practices, it is essential that a sound value base underpins the service. We must not lose sight of the purpose for which the services are provided.

These values – which may also be referred to as principles – can be developed from a number of different sources. Three with which you are likely to be familiar are:

- Underpinning values – Users' Rights from *A Framework for the Development of Standards for the Provision of Domiciliary Care*, produced by the Joint Advisory Group of Domiciliary Care Associations.
- The '0' unit – the value base underpinning the Care sector NVQ awards.
- Principles identified in *Home Life: A code of practice for residential care* and reproduced in *CareFully*. If you have not already done so, you should obtain copies of all three statements, plus the checklists that appear in *CareFully*.

From these and other statements you may have come across, you should be able to develop your own statement of values or principles that apply to the service for which you are responsible. *CareFully* also produces a list of 'rights' for people receiving care. This is very closely aligned to the values, and it is worth recognising that values and principles are meaningless unless people receiving care are able to exercise their 'rights'.

The values and 'rights' cover a wide range of topics; for example, supporting independence, allowing people to take identified risks and maintaining the privacy, dignity and confidentiality of the people receiving care. However, one of the most important areas is that of equality and non-discriminatory practice. You need to decide what your organisation's policy is or will be in relation to providing non-discriminatory services and also the rights of your staff not to be discriminated against in any way. (See later in this chapter and Chapter 4.) If you are the manager of a home care team, you should ensure that your values are consistent with those of the organisation as a whole.

It is possible to consider the provision of care to people as 'just another business'. However, the vast majority of people become involved because of a personal concern for others and a desire to help them when in need. It is the values or principles that underpin the provision of care that distinguish it from any other business.

If you are an owner/manager, you are in a position to influence the values of the whole agency. If you are a manager of a team, you can adapt the values of the organisation as a whole to meet the particular needs of the people you are caring for. If the organisation does not have its own statement of values, you can develop your own and influence the organisation as a whole to adopt them.

It is very easy to develop a statement of values but it is no good at all having values if they are not practised. There are many organisations that do not practise what they preach, and lose credibility as a result. A major factor is to develop the values with input from staff: it is staff who will put them into practice.

The values should underpin and influence practice – the way in which care is provided. The only people in a position to judge whether that actually happens are those who receive care and their family and friends. They must be told about the underpinning values and have the opportunity to comment and give feedback on whether the values are being implemented.

PROVIDING A QUALITY SERVICE

In order to provide a quality service you need to identify standards for its delivery and introduce a system by which you can be assured that the standards are being met, or even surpassed. This is known as quality assurance.

Setting standards

'Standards' is a rather over-worked word at the moment, but don't let that put you off! Dictionary definitions include:

- An accepted or approved example of something against which others are judged or measured
- A level of excellence or quality

The term 'standards' has become synonymous with quality, but that is misleading: standards can be low as well as high. The key is in the setting of the standards. Unless you set standards, the quality of your service cannot be measured and no one will know whether it is of a low or a high quality. You may feel that that is a good thing, but in today's increasingly competitive climate you need to be able to demonstrate the standard of your service.

But beware when setting standards – be realistic. Don't set them so high that they cannot be achieved. This will only bring the standards and your organisation or team into disrepute. You should set achievable standards that will provide targets for staff and encourage and motivate them. When you and your staff have achieved the standards that have been set, they can always be increased so that the overall quality of the service is improved.

There are many examples of standards around at the moment: the Citizen's Charter, the Patient's Charter and the Community Care Charter all set standards, some of which can be relatively meaningless. For example: 'All patients will be seen within 15 minutes of arrival in the clinic' does not necessarily mean that they will be seen by the doctor with whom they have an appointment. They may be seen by the receptionist and left to wait for the doctor but the terms of the standard will have been met.

You will need to set your own standards but you don't have to reinvent the wheel. There are at least two documents that will help you:

- *A Framework for the Development of Standards for the Provision of Domiciliary Care*
- NVQ level 2 and 3 standards for the Care awards

The first document has already been widely used by agencies to set standards. It enables you as a manager to identify both the standards that must be met from the outset and the targets to work towards in the longer term.

The NVQ standards are more generally thought of in the context of obtaining a qualification, and at present that is generally how they are used. However, they also have a much wider application and relevance in that the elements and the performance criteria are standards. Anyone who is assessed as competent is able to perform the task to the specified standards. These then can be used to set performance standards for your staff.

As with the aims and objectives, the standards should be developed in consultation with staff, the people receiving the service and the purchasers of the service. Once standards have been agreed, they should be publicised.

Quality assurance

Quality assurance, or QA as it is commonly referred to, is the process of ensuring that the standards are met. Everyone has a part to play in implementing quality assurance and for assuring the quality of their own work – which is why all staff should be involved in setting the standards. If staff personally 'own' the standards, they are going to want to ensure that their work meets those standards. The main stages of an effective QA system are identified in the following diagram.

You will see from the diagram that much of what we have already covered in this book contributes to the development of a QA system. Chapter 2 considered business planning. In this chapter we have covered the aims, objectives and underpinning values and the setting of standards. Developing operational policies and procedures such as those identified in the rest of this chapter is an essential part of establishing the QA process. Implementation of the policies and procedures helps in assuring the quality of the service being provided.

Developing operational policies and procedures can be the most time-consuming part of the activity, particularly in the initial stages. Beware. It is easy to take on too much work and in the meantime the quality suffers.

Complaints procedures

A complaints procedure is an integral part of an effective QA system. Social services departments are required by law to have a complaints procedure in place, and it is also good practice for other organisations. If you work in an organisation that does not yet have a formal complaints procedure, it is worth looking at your local authority's system to see what it covers and how it works before introducing your own. Their processes may help you avoid reinventing the wheel!

The complaints procedure should be actively promoted to all people receiving care and their personal carers, to purchasers of your services and to your staff. Information leaflets, cards etc should all give details about the procedure. People receiving care should be assured that not only is it *acceptable* for them to complain but it is a *necessary* part of ensuring the quality of your service.

All leaflets giving information of any kind on the service you are providing, including the complaints procedure, should be in a format and style that is easily readable and 'user friendly'. They should be available in the language spoken in their home by the people receiving care and in a tape format for people with visual disabilities. If you have problems with translation, your local authority or Citizens Advice Bureau will be able to advise you.

It is extremely difficult to get people who receive home care to complain, even when they have very good reason to do so. They are normally grateful for the assistance that enables them to continue to live at home, and afraid that the help may be taken away from them if they complain. As a manager you have a responsibility to assure them that this would not happen.

An earlier section of this chapter discussed standards for the delivery of the service. Part of the standard setting should involve the response to and investigation of complaints. You will need to ensure that complaints are acknowledged promptly and investigated as speedily as possible. The number and nature of the complaints must be monitored as part of the QA process so that appropriate action such as staff training may be taken to remedy the situation.

If you are a manager in a private sector agency providing care services on behalf of the local authority, it is likely that, as part of the specification and contract, the authority will require your agency to have a formal complaints procedure. You will also have to provide the authority regularly with a report of the complaints and the action taken.

Confidentiality

Maintaining confidentiality is also an important part of the overall QA process. Home care staff will inevitably be told things by the people they are caring for. You need to be certain that staff will respect the confidence and not pass on information or gossip about their service users and their personal circumstances to third parties. This seems fairly obvious, yet it's all too easy to let slip information about, for example, people's habits, when they are going on holiday or where they keep the door key so that others can let themselves in.

NOTE If you or the home carer has the key to a person's home, mark it with a reference or code number, not the address.

There will, of course, be occasions when home care staff will need to report back information to their line manager for action, thus possibly breaking the rule of confidentiality. Such situations include:

- suspicion of elder abuse;
- deteriorating health, including incontinence, dependence on alcohol, not eating;
- requests from the GP, district nurse to assist with medication;
- onset of mental confusion.

When developing your policy on confidentiality (which could be incorporated into the underpinning values), you also need to identify the circumstances in which information may be passed on to the line manager or another appropriate professional such as the person's GP. These circumstances will normally be ones that threaten the physical or mental health of the individual and put them at risk and where further decisions need to be taken about their care. This distinction needs to be explained to the person receiving care and their relatives. Information should not be passed on to other agencies or professionals without the knowledge and permission of the person concerned.

Your policy on confidentiality should include a warning about the dangers of home care staff becoming too friendly with the people they are caring for and their family. Whilst this may be welcomed by the person needing care, particularly if they are relatively isolated, it can also cause considerable difficulties, increase demands on the home carer and may eventually make the job impossible for them.

As a manager of a home care service, you also have a responsibility to maintain confidentiality under the requirements of the Data Protection Act 1984. This means ensuring that access to personal files (manual and computerised) is restricted to those who need to see the files. It also means that the files must be located in a secure place.

You may wish to insert a clause on confidentiality in your contract or agreement with home care staff.

Handling money, gifts and bequests

Many home care staff will go shopping and collect pensions for the people they are caring for. You must have a clear policy on the procedure to be adopted in these circumstances, which includes:

- accounting for every penny spent;
- handing over receipts;
- keeping a written record of all transactions;
- never mixing personal money with that of the person receiving care.

This is an area in which it is not possible to be too cautious, and clear procedures will protect the home carer as well as the client.

It is natural, though, for people receiving care to want to thank the person who has cared for them, particularly on birthdays and at Christmas. You may decide to have a policy that prohibits home carers from receiving any gifts at all from the people they are caring for. In practice, such a policy is rarely understood by the people making the gift and they can take offence, which places the home carer in a difficult position.

You may therefore consider it more appropriate to have a policy that gifts up to the value of (say) £5 may be accepted and that receipt of such gifts must always be reported to the line manager. (This should avoid the problem that occurred, of the man who gave cars to his home carers!)

Your policy should also deal with legacies and bequests. It must be clear that these should never be accepted, under any circumstances. Obviously, staff should never ask to borrow money nor suggest, even as a joke, that the person they are caring for should leave them money or goods in their will. There are, however, occasions when people decide to do this of their own free will, in gratitude for the care and kindness they have received. If the home carer becomes aware of this, it should be reported to their line manager.

You may wish to include your policies about confidentiality, handling money and gifts, legacies and bequests in a broad Code of Conduct for staff.

RECRUITMENT AND SELECTION

Your organisation should have a clear recruitment and selection policy. It is not that many years since home care jobs in social services departments were advertised in corner shops or were not advertised at all – home carers were recruited by word of mouth from the friends and relatives of staff. In such a situation there is no question of introducing a proper interview and selection process, and mistakes could – and often did – occur.

The recruitment and selection policy should cover the issues identified below. You may find it useful to obtain examples of recruitment and selection policies from other home care providers and from the Social Care Association (SCA), but you should always remember that the policy should reflect the values of your own organisation, not just adopt those of another.

Recruitment and selection policy

This should cover:

- Whether you really need more staff in the first place – what will be the 'added value' to your business?
- Advertising – where posts should be advertised (eg named newspapers and journals, JobCentre, libraries, GP surgeries, 'open days')
- Equal opportunities
- Application forms
- Interview process – including the use of a person specification and other forms to ensure objectivity

- Standard, set questions to ensure equal opportunities
- Training of those involved in the interview process
- References – to be taken up in writing before a formal offer of a post is made
- Procedure for offering a post
- Job description
- Probationary period
- Training and development of staff
- Exit interviews for people who are leaving

Examples of a job description and a person specification for a home care assistant are given in Appendixes 4 and 5. Examples of questions to be used in an interview are listed in Appendix 6.

The recruitment and selection policy should contain a statement to the effect that advertising, recruitment and selection are non-discriminatory in terms of race, gender, colour, religion and sexual orientation. All staff involved in recruitment and selection should be given appropriate training, including the implications of the Sex Discrimination Act 1975 and the Race Relations Act 1976.

Recruitment procedures should be monitored regularly to ensure that the policy is being followed in practice. Social service departments will require evidence that the equal opportunities policy is being implemented by organisations providing home care services on their behalf.

Job descriptions and conditions of employment

You will need to develop clear job descriptions and conditions of employment. The NVQ level 2 standards for care provide a useful means of developing job specifications that directly relate to the training and competence required by home care assistants. It is as important to include in the job description, or as an appendix to it, information about the tasks that home care assistants must *not* perform, as to do so might well invalidate the insurance cover. For example:

- lifting someone out of a bath unaided;
- climbing tall or unsafe step ladders;
- making electrical repairs;

- specified medical activities;
- nursing tasks (eg injections, suppositories, administering controlled drugs).

Conditions of employment must also be clear and non-discriminatory. As well as covering

rates and method of payment	superannuation (if applicable)
annual leave entitlement	sick leave
required training	travel expenses
termination of employment	right to join a trade union
code of dress and conduct	grievance and disciplinary procedures

the conditions of employment should include information on how home care staff are expected to carry out the policies and procedures of the organisation. You may also consider it worth while having a clause concerning confidentiality as part of the conditions of employment.

In order to safeguard the interests of the employing organisation, it is also sensible to include a clause relating to staff leaving and going to work for another home care provider, or working directly for someone who needs care – thus bypassing your agency or organisation. Generally, a three-month period is considered reasonable, with the possibility of compensation if this clause is broken.

Some service providers keep a 'float' of money to cover the home carers' travelling expenses until payment is received. Travelling costs can be an expensive item for home carers and few are willing to admit that they cannot afford to pay for it out of their own pocket until expenses are reimbursed. This can be a disincentive for them to take on emergency work unless they know that they are not, even in the short term, going to have to meet the travel costs themselves.

Training

You must have a clear training policy and a strategy for putting it into practice. The areas that should be covered in the training policy are listed below. The list is not intended to be comprehensive but gives you an indication of the topics to cover.

Sample training policy

Essential training

- Induction into the policies, practices and procedures of the organisation, including the underpinning value base
- Health and safety
- Lifting and manual handling
- Provision of non-discriminatory services
- Legislation and the implication for practice
- Communication skills, including care of people with sensory impairment
- Basic first aid

Desirable training

- NVQ Care awards
- Maintaining continence
- Caring for confused people

Specialist training

- Care of the terminally ill
- Care of people with HIV or AIDS
- Working with people from ethnic minority communities
- Working in dirty and infested homes
- Care of people who have had strokes

Even if you are not able to implement the NVQ Care standards in full, you can still use them to structure and focus staff training, particularly if the standards have been used as a basis when compiling job descriptions and individual units may be credited.

As a manager in the home care service, you might consider obtaining accreditation as an internal assessor for the NVQ Care awards. This would be consistent with the Management standards that identify the development of staff as part of the manager's responsibility. This is explored further in Chapter 7.

Not all training need be undertaken in formal sessions. Much can be achieved in normal staff meetings and supervision sessions, for example updating on the implications of legislation. Costs of time and travel can also be reduced by using open learning packages such as those of the Open University and UNISON. The Joint Initiative for Community Care (JICC) is developing a workbook for home care staff, directly related to the NVQ level 2 Care standards. This should be available in 1996/97.

You should ensure that all staff have equal access to training opportunities. To achieve this you should monitor which staff are receiving training and how often. You also need to identify any barriers to staff taking part in training and find ways that these may be overcome. Obviously in a small organisation it is difficult, time consuming and expensive to undertake the full range of training. However, local authority social services departments are being encouraged by the Department of Health to open up their training to independent and voluntary sector organisations.

Some agencies encourage staff to attend training by paying them an extra 5p an hour on their normal wage, on the understanding that they will attend training. They are not paid, though, for the time spent in the training itself.

LEGISLATION, INCLUDING HEALTH AND SAFETY

You must have policies, and procedures in place to implement them, reflecting the key areas of legislation:

- Employment law, including the Sex Discrimination Act 1975, Race Relations Act 1976 and EC Regulations, particularly that relating to the employment of part-time staff.
- Data protection, including the Data Protection Act 1984 and the Personal Protection Act 1989.
- Health and safety, including lifting and manual handling.

All are important, but the issues of the health and safety of home care staff are particularly important because failure to implement the requirements of the legislation result directly in many days of sick leave. Back problems and injury caused by incorrect lifting and handling are by far the greatest cause of both home care staff being off work and insurance claims under employer liability.

In relation to employment law and data protection, most of the policy and procedures will relate to your, or a colleague's, function as a manager. However, part of the policy should cover the implications of the legislation for the way in which home care staff work. As a manager you will need to ensure, through staff meetings and regular supervision, that the legal requirements are put into practice.

Health and Safety at Work etc Act 1984

Do not forget the EC Manual Handling Regulations 1993! This is a most important area in which clear policies and practices are essential.

Before allocating home care staff to work in a person's home, the risks and hazards in that home must be assessed. This assessment used to be undertaken by the home care manager when responding to a new referral. However, now that assessment and commissioning of services within many local authorities are separate from the actual provision of services, risk assessment should be undertaken as part of the comprehensive assessment of need and built into the care package.

The reality is that the risk assessment is still often undertaken by home care managers. This is either because it has not been done as part of the care management and commissioning process or because managers have a responsibility to their staff – which means that they must apprise themselves of the home circumstances and risks associated with it, before sending staff into the home.

The risks usually identified are common household risks such as overloaded electric sockets, frayed wires, trailing flexes and worn carpets. Sometimes they require immediate action; for example, infestation of mice or cockroaches.

The assessment of risk should include manual handling but this assessment is usually undertaken separately. An example of a manual handling risk assessment form is given in Appendix 2. Some 30 per cent of injuries are caused by incorrect lifting. The current legal position is that no one should attempt to lift, carry or move a load so heavy that it is likely to cause injury.

The Manual Handling Directive requires hoists to be installed when people need to be lifted, for example, in and out of a bath or wheelchair.

If people are able to help themselves to some extent, it may be possible for two people to assist with the lifting, but only after they have received proper training.

Training in lifting and handling is absolutely essential and should be part of the induction programme. The training should then be reinforced periodically with refresher and updating sessions, and be a regular item on the agenda of team meetings.

Training should also cover the implications of the Control of Substances Harmful to Health Act (COSHH) to ensure that staff know how to handle and store safely any hazardous substances, and are up to date regarding the control of infectious diseases such as hepatitis B and the human immuno-deficiency virus (HIV). If you work in a small organisation and it is going to be difficult for you to put on such training, contact your local social services department as they run this and similar programmes all the time.

You should advise home care staff to keep their tetanus injections up to date and that they can, if they wish, ask their GP for immunisation against hepatitis B.

A contentious subject is the involvement of home care staff in helping people take their medication at the right time. Because they are often the ones most frequently in contact with the people they are caring for, home care staff come under considerable pressure to become involved – by GPs, district nurses, relatives and the individuals themselves. Yet, if anything were to go wrong, they could be blamed. Your organisation must have a clear policy about the extent and circumstances of the home carer's involvement. There should be clear instructions for the home carer, which include reporting back to their line manager when the involvement is first proposed and seeking their agreement.

Your policy on the involvement of staff in helping with medication should be clearly relayed to people needing care, their families, GP practices in your area and local authority purchasers of home care. All medicines are potentially harmful if misused and care must be taken in their storage, administration and control.

As a manager it is in your interest to ensure that staff follow the procedures in relation to health and safety in general and to lifting and handling in particular. Not following the procedures can cause harm to the person needing the care as well as to the home carer. Even if you do not directly employ home carers yourself because they are self-employed, you will still have to find someone to replace a person who is unable to work because of an injury sustained in the course of their job.

You must, by law, have a procedure for reporting all accidents, however minor. (An example of an accident report form is given in Appendix 3.) The accident must then be recorded in an accident record book which is held centrally. All serious accidents must be reported to the Health and Safety Executive. If you are providing home care services on behalf of the social services department, they too will want to regularly inspect your accident record book.

Unfortunately, attacks on staff are becoming more frequent. You should have a procedure for home care staff to report physical, sexual or verbal assaults received in the course of their work and for appropriate action to be taken. An incident report form should be completed so that there is a permanent record, allowing the situation to be monitored. Some organisations take the precaution of issuing mobile phones, bleeps or panic alarms to staff who work late at night.

All aspects of the health and safety policy and procedures require careful and regular monitoring to ensure that the procedures are being followed and to take appropriate corrective action if necessary.

One of the dilemmas inherent within the health and safety legislation is how to balance the rights of the individual person to live their own chosen lifestyle (hazards and all) with complying with the law. Even if the person needing care accepts the degree of risk – which is their right – you have a responsibility for the safety of the person providing care. Ultimately, if the risk is too great, you have the right to refuse to allow staff to work in a hazardous environment. (See also Chapter 6.)

Emergency procedures

You must have a clear policy and procedure for dealing with emergencies. This policy will complement the health and safety policy and should be covered within induction training. Emergencies include:

- Finding the person unwell or collapsed
- Finding the person dead

- Unable to gain access to the home
- Home carer unable to turn up
- Fire or flood
- Burglary

Home care staff should always be informed if the person has a condition such as diabetes which could result in their finding the person in a coma.

By far the most common emergencies are medical but your procedures also need to take account of other situations. Telephone numbers should be clearly displayed in the person's home for use in an emergency and should include the number of the GP and nearest friend or relative.

Health and safety and emergencies are also covered fully in *CareFully*.

KEY POINTS

Your organisation, section or team needs policies and procedures on:

- Aims and objectives of the organisation – business targets.
- Underpinning values.
- Standards for delivery of the service.
- Quality assurance.
- Complaints and compliments.
- Code of conduct for staff:
  - confidentiality (including Data Protection Act and circumstances in which information should be passed on);
  - handling money;
  - gifts and bequests.
- Recruitment and selection, including the implications of employment law.
- Equal opportunities and non-discriminatory practice.
- Training.
- Health and safety, including:
  - lifting and handling;
  - infectious diseases;
  - administration of medication.
- Emergencies.

4 Managing People

This chapter relates to Management standards:

M1 4.1, 4.2, 5.1, 5.2, 6.1–6.4, 7.1, 7.5, 7.6

M2 5.1–5.3, 6.1, 6.2, 6.4, 7.1–7.4, 8.1, 8.5, 8.6

The provision of home care is a 'people orientated' business – people receive the service and people provide it. It is therefore essential that all aspects of managing people are undertaken with skill and sensitivity.

RECRUITMENT AND SELECTION

There are a number of stages in the recruitment and selection process, as shown in the diagram opposite. Each of these stages is discussed in the following paragraphs.

As a manager you cannot afford to make any mistakes in the recruitment and selection of staff. First of all, it is a lengthy and time-consuming process that costs the organisation a considerable amount of money – so you don't want to have to repeat it too often. Perhaps more important, though, is that if you make the wrong decision and appoint someone who proves unsuitable for the work (for whatever reason), the people receiving the service may suffer and ultimately it may affect the reputation and therefore the income of the whole organisation.

So you need to get it right first time!

RECRUITMENT AND SELECTION PROCESS

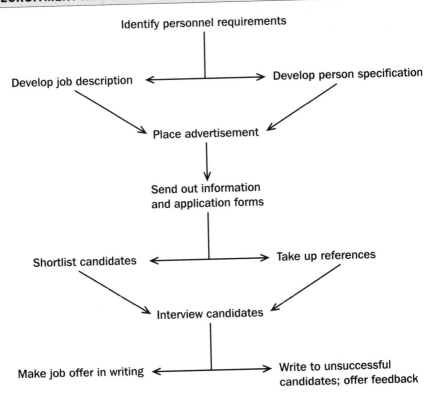

Define personnel requirements

The number of people you recruit will depend on the volume of business and the caseload. However, the volume of business you can handle will depend upon the number of home carers you have available to provide the care. It is a circular dilemma – the two factors are completely inter-dependent.

The starting point should be your business plan – identifying the number of people you need in order to achieve the objectives and targets specified in the business plan.

You may need at this point to decide on the average size of the caseload (ie the number of people receiving care from each home carer). The specific number will vary, depending upon factors such as:

- the complexity and intensity of the service provided;
- the number of hours worked by the home carer;
- where people needing care live and travelling times involved.

However, an estimate of the average number of people cared for by each carer will help you to calculate your staffing requirements.

It may be that you will not require all staff at the same time. However, because of the cost of recruitment, it may be worth while considering recruiting staff 'in one go' and phasing in over (say) a six-month period when they will actually start work, or keeping a 'pool' of suitable people you can call on when you need them. You may risk losing potential staff to other organisations but this may be preferable to repeating the recruitment and selection process too frequently.

Defining personnel requirements is not only about deciding the number of staff your organisation requires; it is also about deciding whether those staff should have any particular personal features, skills or experience. You should analyse the nature of your current workforce and compare this with the needs of people currently receiving care services from your organisation and your future potential market. This process should identify whether there are any significant gaps that you need to fill from your recruitment and selection process. For example:

- Does your workforce reflect an ethnic mix similar to the people currently receiving care and the geographical area you serve – or do you need to recruit more people from ethnic minority communities?
- Are you providing more intensive care services? Do you need people with nursing or nursing auxiliary experience and qualifications?
- Are you providing a flexible service, 24 hours a day, seven days a week? Do you need to recruit more people who are willing and able to work flexible and unsocial hours?
- Are all your home carers women? Would it be useful, to meet the needs of some of the people needing care, if you were able to recruit some male home carers? (This is often a practical solution when female home carers are harassed by male service users.)

It is becoming increasingly expected by both the people receiving care and the purchasers of care on their behalf that, wherever possible, you will try to match the home carer to the cultural and religious needs of people needing care. To do this you need to recruit staff who have a wide range of attributes and abilities.

NOTE   Use the NVQ level 2 and 3 Care standards as a checklist. Going through the units, elements and performance criteria that are relevant to your home care business will help identify any gaps in the skills, attributes and competence of your current staff group.

Having defined your personnel requirements, you are prepared to move on to the next stage in the recruitment and selection process.

Job descriptions

Job descriptions list the tasks that you expect staff to perform and to what standard. An example of a job description for a home carer is given in Appendix 4.

The NVQ level 2 and 3 Care standards mentioned in the Note, above, can be used to develop the job description. You can then relate the activities that staff are required to carry out to the standards of competence and thus identify the training needs.

If you are providing different types of care services, of different degrees of complexity and intensity, you may need to develop different job descriptions. However, it is probably sensible and easier to have a core job description that is common to all; you can then add to and vary it to meet more specialist needs and requirements as necessary.

Person specifications

Person specifications list the attributes, skills and knowledge that you require of the staff you wish to recruit. Normally, person specifications are divided into two elements – essential and desirable. An example of a person specification relating to the job description will be found in Appendix 5.

It should be possible to draw up the person specification from the definition of personnel requirements undertaken at the beginning of the recruitment process. There may be variations according to the different types of care services or different people needing care but, as with the job description, it is advisable to have a core person specification that can be varied to meet particular needs.

Check that both the job description and the person specification meet the requirements of the organisation's equal opportunities policy. Make sure that you have not inadvertently excluded a potential applicant by asking for unnecessary skills and experience.

Place advertisements and send out information

Before placing the advertisement, research the local labour market to find out the employment situation and the competition (and their wage rates if possible). Visit the local JobCentre, look in local newspapers, and contact other organisations providing different forms of home care service through the local *Yellow Pages* directory. Local Training and Enterprise Councils (TECs) should have information on the local labour market, as should the Economic Development Unit of your local authority – if they have one.

The definition of the personnel requirements, the job description and the person specification should provide you with plenty of information for the advertisement. Advertisements should be clear and concise. The main purpose of the business should be outlined, and the underpinning values to which your organisation subscribes. Attention should be drawn to the key attributes, skills and experience you are seeking.

Decide where you are going to advertise your vacancies. The local JobCentre and the local newspaper are the most obvious locations but, if you wish to recruit in a particular geographic location, you may wish to consider other possibilities such as a local library, local shop or even a GP practice.

Misleading advertisements that are poorly researched will result in either too many applicants, in which case you will have to spend time rejecting large numbers, or too few applying. High staff turnover is costly and will not enhance the reputation of your organisation with either purchasers or people needing care.

Decide what information you are going to send out to applicants. At the very least, there should be the following documentation:

- Background information about your organisation and the service you provide
- Examples of policy statements
- Job description
- Person specification
- Application form

Application forms should not request any additional information that is contrary to the equal opportunities policy (eg marital status, number of dependants).

The application form should be 'user friendly', not intimidating, and should invite applicants to list their skills, knowledge and experience under the same headings as the person specification. This will save you time by helping you to compare candidates' experience more easily. Specify that the application form *must* be completed, even if the candidate has their own CV; a generalised CV will not relate to the particular requirements of home care. Invite possible applicants to meet you or telephone you to find out more about the work.

At least two references should be requested – one being from a previous employer if possible or from the equivalent person if they have worked as a volunteer.

A record should be kept of the names and addresses of all the people who are sent details of the post and noted with those who actually complete and return the application form. This enables you to compare the number of enquiries with the ones that are translated into applications. A relatively low proportion (under 60 per cent) suggests that there may be a problem with the advertisement that prompted the enquiry in the first place. For example, the advertisement may not adequately reflect the nature of the work and, after the initial enquiry, potential applicants are put off when they read the more detailed information.

In some parts of the country it is extremely difficult to recruit the right staff. You will need to find ways to attract them to your organisation rather than going for any other form of work.

Shortlisting candidates for interview

Shortlisting is the process by which you will match candidates' skills, knowledge etc with the requirements identified in the person specification. People who are shortlisted should be those who most closely meet the requirements of the specification.

NOTE Weight the attributes, skills and experience by placing them in order of importance and allocating a number for each. For example, ability to get on with people scores 10 if you feel that this is the most important skill; experience of caring for older people, 9; and so on. This simple scoring mechanism helps differentiate between applicants who meet most, if not all, of the requirements of the person specification and is more objective than using subjective terms such as good or poor. It will also be useful in the interview itself and will make it easier for you to give objective feedback to unsuccessful candidates (eg 'you didn't score very highly on . . .').

References

If at all possible, references should be taken up *before* the interview. When seeking references, send details of the post that the applicant has applied for and be as specific as possible about the information you want. For example:

- general suitability for the work;
- trustworthiness;
- timekeeping;
- physical and mental health;
- length of time and capacity in which the referee has known the applicant;
- date for the return of the reference.

Remember to enclose a stamped addressed envelope for them to return the reference.

It is always a good idea to follow up written references with a telephone call to identify forgeries. (Yes, it has been known, and you can't afford to take chances with the safety of your customers!) Unfortunately, it is not generally possible to have a police check undertaken on the record of the vast majority of home care staff, unless they are likely to be working with children. This makes it even more important that you undertake a very thorough check on the validity of the references.

Interview candidates

You will need to apply your equal opportunities policy to the interview process. Interviews should take place in the office of the manager of the home care service or some other suitable premises such as an interview or seminar room. They should not be held in more casual surroundings.

Allow at least 30 minutes for each applicant. Try to make the environment as friendly and relaxed as possible in order to put the applicant at their ease: do not place a formal desk between the interviewer and the applicant, use easy rather than upright chairs, and so on. You may consider involving more than one interviewer in the process to ensure objectivity and independence.

Develop a list of standard questions beforehand based on the person specification and the job description. The same questions should be asked of each applicant and should encourage them to give examples of their attributes, skills, experience and so on. The weighting of the requirements for the post, undertaken at the shortlisting stage, can be usefully applied again to assesses objectively the relative merits of each applicant. An example of a list of standard questions appears in Appendix 6.

Candidates should be encouraged to ask questions about the work and the organisation. Tell all applicants when they can expect to hear whether or not they have been successful.

Informing candidates

Let successful candidates know the outcome as soon as possible by telephoning them and then following up with a formal letter giving them a proposed starting date and a contract of employment to sign, if appropriate. (But see also 'Medical checks', below.)

Send successful candidates any information on the organisation, its policies and practices that they have not already received (eg terms and conditions of service, information on staff development and training, code of conduct).

Write to unsuccessful candidates telling them why they were not successful on this occasion. You may wish to offer to place them on a list for the future if the organisation expands further.

Medical checks

Because of the strenuous nature of home care work, it is essential that the physical capabilities of each successful candidate are properly and independently assessed. This will help to ensure that staff are not placed in situations that exceed their personal physical limits, and should prevent the loss of time and money dealing with sickness absence later on.

New staff should be required to complete a medical questionnaire designed to identify any particular physical or medical risks. (It is worth checking the content of the questionnaire with your insurance company to ensure that there are no loop-holes.) If there is any doubt, you may wish to request that a full medical examination be undertaken (at your cost). Local authorities often use the services of an occupational physician in the local health authority or NHS Trust. Offers of employment should then be made formally only when medical clearance has been obtained.

Probationary period

It is sensible to make each appointment subject to the satisfactory completion of a probationary period lasting not less than three months and not more than six. This gives you an opportunity to judge the suitability of the new recruit in practice and also for them to gain experience and decide whether this is the job for them.

TRAINING AND STAFF DEVELOPMENT

All organisations should have a policy for training and developing staff and a strategy for translating the policy into action. The training policy should cover a planned induction programme, essential areas of training, desirable areas and specialist training.

All staff will require some training and development, whatever their experience and qualifications. Training of staff is an integral part of providing a quality service, and is justifiable in those terms even though the cost of training will be reflected in the unit cost charged for your service.

Although purchasers may initially have been encouraged to contract with the cheapest services, many are now becoming more sophisticated and are willing to pay a higher price for a higher quality service, and that includes trained staff.

Smaller organisations may have difficulty in providing the full range of training and staff development opportunities. One way of overcoming this is to link up with the local authority social services department, which is encouraged by the Department of Health to open up its programmes to agencies in the private and voluntary sectors.

Other practical options include the use of open learning material such as that published by UNISON (the OPAL 2 package) and the Open University, and of workbooks such as that currently being developed by JICC specifically for home care staff. The earlier book in this series, *CareFully: A guide for home care assistants*, has also been used successfully by many organisations to train staff. Another possibility is to join forces with other small organisations in your area but this may prove difficult if the element of competition is too great.

If yours is a very small organisation, give your staff literature from local colleges, the Red Cross and St John's Ambulance, and suggest that they use these training courses.

The particular difficulties of providing training for staff who are self-employed are recognised. One way to overcome this may be to pay an additional amount per hour – say 5p – on top of the normal rate, on the understanding that they will attend relevant training in their own time.

Induction training

You should consider carefully the structure and format of the induction process. Cramming it all into the first three hours on the first day is rarely helpful and results in new staff forgetting more than they retain. Topics to be included in an induction programme are:

- Aims and objectives of the organisation
- Underpinning values
- Policies and procedures, including equal opportunities
- Terms and conditions of employment

- Completion of timesheets and travel claim forms
- Monitoring and supervision
- Personal care and hygiene
- Basic lifting and handling techniques
- Standards of work to be attained
- Issue of identification badge with photograph of the home carer
- Issue of protective clothing, including overall and rubber gloves (to be signed for, with rules about misuse of uniform)
- Introduction to other staff
- On-the-job training and work experience

A handbook should be provided for each member of staff, to include personal copies of policies, training handouts, etc. The development of the handbook provides a useful *aide memoir* for home care staff and managers alike. The final session in induction training should be a 'comeback' session, running through all the documents given, and asking carers to sign that they have read the policies and are familiar with the procedures.

NOTE   It is often better to develop a phased induction programme over a specified time (eg the first two weeks of employment), introducing the recruit to a new area of activity each day. It is also helpful if they can have the opportunity at the very beginning to work alongside or 'shadow' an experienced home carer.

Essential training

An induction programme on its own is rarely going to be sufficient training for most new employees because it will only cover most topics on a superficial basis. A planned programme of further training is required, covering the topics listed below:

- Introduction to relevant legislation
- Health and safety – general
- Lifting and handling, including manual handling and back care
- Accidents and emergencies
- Basic first aid
- Health and hygiene, including handling food
- The process of ageing

- The effects of common diseases and disabilities
- Providing people-centred services, including care plans and basic communication skills

These topics are essential because they are either required by law or provide essential knowledge and skills that will enable new staff to work effectively. Without staff undertaking the essential areas of training it will be unlikely, if not impossible, to maintain standards and deliver a high quality service. Some of these topics may be combined; for example, health and safety with accidents and emergencies, or the process of ageing with the effects of common diseases and disabilities.

Although the values underpinning the provision of services, organisational policies and practices and the standards of service required will have been covered as part of the induction programme, they should also be an integral part of each and every training activity. No opportunity should be lost to reinforce the message.

Desirable and specialist areas of training

Not all areas of training and staff development are essential. Some are desirable in that they contribute to the knowledge and competence of home care staff and help raise the overall standard of the service that is provided. Specialist areas of training and development include topics or situations that require the response of a specially trained member of staff but are not needed by all staff.

Desirable training

- NVQ level 2 Care award
- Maintaining continence
- Dealing with aggressive behaviour
- Caring for confused people
- Maintaining independence

Specialist training

- Caring for people from ethnic minority communities
- Caring for people with HIV or AIDS

- Caring for terminally ill people
- The tasks of a nursing auxiliary (eg changing dressings, pressure sores)
- Working in dirty or infested homes

Obtaining the full NVQ Care award at level 2 is undoubtedly desirable but many organisations, including those that are well established and have a considerable number of employees, find the cost of putting home care staff through the NVQ prohibitive. There are problems in bringing staff together on a regular basis to undertake any training, group discussion or feedback from open learning approaches. Nevertheless, these problems are not insurmountable.

The greatest difficulty arises in relation to the assessment of competence in practice. Apart from the ethical considerations raised by invading the privacy of someone's home, the cost of assessing competence in practice on a one-to-one basis is significant. Some agencies have tried to overcome these problems by bringing home care staff into residential homes and day centres to undertake the assessment, but even this approach has yet to make a significant impact on the total number of home care staff eligible for the NVQ award.

One organisation – the Joint Initiative for Community Care – is developing a workbook for home care staff directly related to the NVQ level 2 standards. Completion of the exercises in the workbook should provide portfolio evidence for assessment of competence and thus reduce (although not entirely replace) the volume of competence that must be assessed in practice in the workplace.

Do you need dedicated training staff?

The answer to that question is an emphatic '*no*', but it is the reason that many organisations give for not implementing an effective strategy for staff development and training.

The training and development of staff should be the responsibility of line managers and incorporated in their day-to-day work, supervision and management practice. This integrated approach to the management and development of staff is endorsed by the NVQ level 4 and level 5 Management standards, in which two of the elements are:

- Develop and improve teams through planning and activities.
- Identify, review and improve development activities for individuals.

The introduction of the Care awards has led line managers to obtain NVQ awards as internal assessors. This should be encouraged because it reinforces the manager's role and responsibility for developing staff. Some people argue that there is not enough time to undertake the management task and fulfil the assessor role, but that is because the latter is still seen as an extra rather than an integral part of the management task.

One of the major advantages of managers assuming this role is that it enables them to identify the areas in which their staff are not yet competent and to take appropriate action. By assuming responsibility for the development of staff, line managers will themselves become more effective managers. However, managers are not necessarily automatically good trainers and will themselves need training and support. The NVQ Management standards should help here.

There will of course be a need for specialist training staff, particularly in some of the areas of specialised training – but lack of training expertise should not become an excuse for line managers not becoming involved with the development of their staff. After all, a strong team equals a strong organisation!

Some organisations have achieved success in NVQs in home care by training senior and experienced home care staff as assessors. Peer group assessment promotes and supports good practice and is a practical way of reducing the assessment load of any one manager.

MANAGEMENT OF STAFF

As a manager of home care staff, you need to be aware of the issues that are involved in the management of a largely untrained workforce, the members of which generally work alone, unsupervised, in somebody's private home. Although home care staff operate in relative isolation from their colleagues, they should not be expected to work in a vacuum, and ways should be found to overcome the isolation.

You have a responsibility to the people who are receiving your care services, and to your employing organisation, to be as sure as possible in the circumstances that the decisions that your staff take every day – working on their own with no one by them to refer to for guidance or information – will be the right decisions. You also need to be reasonably certain that your staff are providing a quality service and are working to the required standard. Failure to do so could, ultimately, place the contract in jeopardy.

There are various ways of reducing the isolation. Assuming responsibility for developing and assessing the competence of staff through the NVQ process was discussed in the previous section, whilst the development of underpinning values, policies and procedures discussed in Chapter 3 provides an operational framework for practice. Managers have a responsibility to ensure that all home care staff are totally familiar with the policies and procedures of the organisation. This and other methods of managing and supervising the work of staff are summarised below.

- Ensure that all home care staff are familiar with the policies and procedures of the organisation.
- Issue staff with a staff handbook.
- Develop a phased induction programme for new members.
- Ensure that quality assurance systems are in place.
- Hold regular (weekly, monthly) team meetings to discuss specific issues and provide group supervision.
- Have regular one-to-one supervision sessions (monthly if possible; every three months is probably realistic).
- Carry out irregular 'spot checks' on home care staff when they are providing care, and give them feedback.
- Introduce consumer satisfaction surveys.
- Undertake internal assessment of competence for NVQ.
- Provide 'out of hours' support.
- Introduce informal processes such as encouraging staff to talk about their work over coffee/tea when they come to the office to deliver timesheets, collect wages, etc.
- Introduce an annual appraisal system.

Team meetings can be used for a wide range of purposes. Not only do they reduce isolation and provide peer group support but they can also be used to explore particular issues and consider good practice. They can provide an opportunity to develop staff.

Although it is not possible regularly to supervise staff in the workplace, arrangements should be made to visit them in the home from time to time. This should be by agreement of the member of staff and a request made in writing to the person receiving care. This is also an opportunity to talk to the service user and find out how they feel about the service they are receiving. Examples of the questions you can ask the person receiving care are:

- Do you have all the written information you need about the service?
- Do you have the name and address of your home carer, care manager or any other person to contact in an emergency?
- Is the service provided on the days and at the time that you want it?
- What does your home carer call you? Is this what you want to be called?
- Does the home carer ask you what you want done?
- Are you told in good time if the home carer is unable to come to you, or is going to be late?
- Does the home carer talk to you about things you want to talk about?
- Is there any way that you think the service you receive could be improved?

From time to time it is appropriate to undertake unannounced 'spot checks', particularly if you have any concerns or doubts about the quality of the service being provided.

Minutes should be taken of formal meetings, including one-to-one supervision sessions and regular team meetings. Any decisions made should also be recorded. Notes of supervision sessions should be signed by both parties.

With the emphasis now on social service departments purchasing home care from a wide range of providers, there is some concern that home care staff may not be spending the contracted length of time in a person's home. This is leading to the introduction of automated time-recording systems (based either on barcodes and 'swipe' pens or on existing alarm systems) to enable a check to be made of the actual time spent providing care.

Maintaining the health of staff

As the manager of staff you have a responsibility to maintain their well-being. After all, if they become sick and are unable to work, it is not only they who will suffer; so will the people they are caring for, and it will cause you, the manager, considerable inconvenience.

Watch out for signs of fatigue, stress or too close involvement and identification with someone they are caring for within the members of your team. All these signs could indicate the beginnings of a problem. Be aware when one of the people receiving care has died and provide counselling for the member of staff, particularly if they have been caring for the person for a number of years. The work of a home carer can be emotionally stressful and draining.

As well as providing one-to-one support when needed, remember that regular team meetings are an opportunity to provide mutual support and assistance.

Remind staff to keep all inoculations such as tetanus and, if necessary, hepatitis B up to date. In winter it is advisable to suggest that staff have influenza injections to protect both themselves and the people they are caring for.

Staff rotas

Paper-based systems are effective but can become unwieldy and inflexible if the number of service users increases. Consider an off-the-shelf computer software package that can be adapted to meet your particular requirements – but remember to ensure that the package includes a telephone helpline.

Although it is possible to develop your own software system, it is not a feasible or economic proposition for most home care managers. It is far better to buy an existing and proven package. Ask around to identify those which people have found most user-friendly.

Working out the rotas can take as much as one day a week, depending on the number and reliability of your staff and the number of people receiving care. Build the time into your work schedule on a regular daily or weekly basis to suit your timetable. If you are running a small business, it is tempting to work out the rotas in your spare time at weekends, but this could lead to stress and overload if you do not make time to switch off from the work.

Many social services departments are moving away from the provision of a home care service only between 9am and 5pm, Monday to Friday, towards a more flexible in-house service, 24 hours a day, seven days a week, to meet users' needs. Developing such a flexible service requires the sensitive introduction of shift work. The two most common patterns are rotating or rolling shifts, in which everyone takes it in turns to work the different shifts, and static shifts, in which staff decide which shifts they wish to work on a regular basis.

Rotating shifts are generally used in residential homes and in hospitals. They are not popular with people receiving care in their own homes because they do not see the same home carer on a regular basis. Nor are rotating shifts generally popular with staff because of difficulty in fitting them into home circumstances. Indeed, many home carers left residential or hospital work to get away from rotating shifts.

Static shifts, on the other hand, have two advantages. The first is the continuity provided by the same home carer looking after the same people at the same time; the other is that the home carer becomes familiar more easily with the particular home circumstances of their 'regular' service users.

A 24-hour service must be backed up by a corresponding support system for staff. Out of normal office hours, an 'on-call' system will be required, and staff will need to know who is 'on call', when, and how to contact them.

Disciplinary and grievance procedures

You need to ensure that your organisation has a disciplinary and a grievance procedure in place. Hopefully, if you recruit and select your staff appropriately, you will hardly ever have to invoke disciplinary measures; nevertheless, you do need the procedure.

There are various degrees of offence that may require disciplinary action to be taken. For example, failure to:

- follow procedures;
- provide care of the required standard;
- take due care and attention.

Provided that it does not result in harm to the person receiving care or to any other person, these matters are best dealt with through one-to-one supervision and a period of close monitoring of performance and refresher training.

The formal disciplinary procedure should be invoked for more serious offences such as breach of confidentiality, making false claims of extra time with the service user (fraud), placing the health and safety of the person needing care at risk or theft. Theft or fraud should always result in dismissal if proven. An example of a disciplinary procedure is given in Appendix 8.

The grievance procedure is invoked by staff if they consider that they have been treated unfairly. Hopefully, if you manage effectively and secure the confidence of your staff, the procedure will rarely, if ever, be used.

Exit interviews

It is good practice to undertake exit interviews when staff leave the organisation. This should provide you with valuable feedback; even if the member of staff is leaving for personal reasons or to develop their career, you should take the opportunity to ask them if there was anything in the organisation that they were unhappy with or gave them cause for concern.

You should keep a record of the reasons why people leave. This may indicate over time whether a pattern emerges; for example, your staff being 'poached' by another home care organisation.

KEY POINTS

- Define your personnel requirements – mistakes in recruitment and selection can be expensive.
- Use the NVQ level 2 and 3 Care standards as a tool to help you develop the job description.
- Ensure equity in the interviewing process.
- Always take up references, and follow up reference letters with a personal telephone call.

- Explore the possibility of linking with other agencies such as the local social services department to help with training.

- Find other cost-effective ways of training staff.

- Hold regular meetings with your home care staff to reduce isolation and to help you ensure that they are working to the required standard.

- Hold regular supervision sessions with staff.

- Make occasional 'spot check' visits to home carers at work, as well as planned visits. Clear with the service user in advance that this is acceptable.

5 Managing the Contract

This chapter relates to Management standards:

M1 1.1, 1.2, 3.2, 8.1, 8.2

M2 1.1, 1.5, 2.1–2.4, 3.1, 3.2, 4.1, 4.2, 9.1–9.3

The community care legislation envisaged local authority social services departments becoming 'enabling' organisations, purchasing services on behalf of people with care needs, from a wide range of organisations in the private and voluntary sectors as well as from their own 'in-house' units providing care. This development was given added impetus in England through the Special Transitional Grant (STG), 85 per cent of which had to be spent in the independent sector. The independent sector was defined as non-local authority and thus included NHS Trusts.

The purchase of services from organisations outside the public sector has led to the introduction of a 'contract culture'. The principal features may be identified as:

- A significant rise in the number of provider organisations in the private and voluntary sectors.
- Increasing competition for business.
- The development of specifications for the delivery of services.
- The introduction of a tendering process.
- Balancing the cost with the quality of the service provided: the higher the quality required, the greater the cost.
- Contracts being issued for the provision of care services on behalf of the local authority (including contracts for social services provider units).

The introduction of Compulsory Competitive Tendering (CCT) within local authorities in the 1980s for activities such as catering and refuse collection has made authorities more familiar with the overall contracting process.

Before the implementation of the NHS and Community Care Act, social service departments were familiar with negotiating and developing service level agreements but not with the full contracting process. Most departments are now on a fast learning curve and are finding that the experience gained in contracting for some services, such as refuse collection, does not automatically apply to the provision of more personal and less specific services such as home care.

As a manager of care services – whichever sector you work in – you need to become increasingly familiar with all aspects of the contracting process. It is highly recommended that you obtain a copy of *Guidance on Contracting for Domiciliary and Day Care Services,* produced by AMA/ACC/ADSS. It contains much useful information on contracting in home care, which it would be pointless, and a waste of effort, to duplicate in its entirety in *Managing CareFully.* If, when you finish reading this chapter, you wish to find out more, there is a unit on contracting and tendering for service managers in OPAL 2 Module 1 published by UNISON.

TYPES OF CONTRACT

There are three main types of contract currently used by local authorities, although inevitably it is possible to find variations on all of them. The three main types are:

- Spot contracts or price by case
- Block contracts
- Cost and volume contracts

The type of contract used by purchasers or commissioners of home care will depend on a number of local factors, including the number and type of organisations providing it, the relative cost of the services, the nature of demand and the level of need. Most local authorities use a combination of all three types of contract.

Spot contracts or price by case

This is the most common form of contract used to purchase home care services from private sector agencies. It is usually used by those responsible for the care management or commissioning function at a local level, responsible for assessing need, putting together the range of services required to meet those needs (the packages of care), and commissioning and contracting for services from one or more providers of care, on behalf of a specific person.

The cost and level of service for spot contracts are agreed on a case by case basis and no two contracts need be exactly the same. They usually involve:

- A new contract written for each service provided.
- Standard conditions which the service provider signs each time.
- A pre-purchase agreement (which establishes the option to purchase).

This agreement is detailed and is signed. It is then possible later to issue simplified forms of the contract for each spot purchase. An example of a pre-purchase agreement may be found in the AMA/ACC/ADSS Guidance referred to above.

The advantage of spot purchasing is that it can be developed to meet specific, individual needs and is therefore 'needs-led'. The disadvantage, particularly for a manager of home care services, is that the level and volume of spot contracts are unpredictable and so there is little security associated with them. They may thus discourage new providers from entering the market.

From the perspective of the local authority purchaser of home care services, spot contracting, whilst providing a great deal of flexibility in responding to people's needs, also creates a diverse and fragmented market in which it is very difficult, if not impossible, to monitor individual contracts.

Block contracts

Block contracts are agreements with a fixed payment for a specified level of service. They have the advantage of providing a greater degree of certainty and predictability for both the commissioners and the service providers. Those responsible for commissioning care are able to request home care service from the block contract that has already been placed.

Most social services departments have so far only entered into block contracts for home care with their own in-house provider service. Over time, however, as the number of contracts for home care increases, a certain level of block contracting is likely to be introduced in many authorities. Social services departments are likely to enter into block contracts with a limited number of approved provider organisations (see the section on p 80 on registration and accreditation).

Small block contracts may encourage providers to enter the market because the block contract guarantees a certain level of income. They also encourage banks to lend money.

The principal disadvantage of block contracts is that they tend to be service-led rather than needs-led. In addition, local authorities have to be certain that they have not contracted for a block of care that is greater in volume than what is actually required. Otherwise they will be paying for services that are not required and not delivered.

Cost and volume contracts

These are a combination of spot and block contracts and have the advantage of offering both certainty and flexibility. Cost and volume contracts normally set a minimum guaranteed volume of business for an agreed cost. The contract then identifies the basis on which additional units of service, in excess of the agreed minimum, may be purchased. It also specifies the price for each additional unit of service.

Cost and volume contracts have advantages for the local authority because they eliminate the danger of contracting for a greater volume of service than is actually required.

Individual service contracts

These contracts are drawn up for specific individual cases. The contract should, ideally, involve the person receiving the care as well as the purchaser of the care and the service provider.

An individual service contract should reflect the content of the individual care plan and the pre-purchase agreement. Details such as the time the service is to be provided, the standard to which it is provided, conditions regarding insurance, additional costs and services, how charges are to be collected and termination of contract should all be included.

There is not a lot of difference between individual service contracts and spot contracts except that the first are generally more tailored to the individual person needing care.

REGISTRATION AND ACCREDITATION SCHEMES

How do purchasers of home care decide which service providers to use? Unlike residential care, which is regulated by the Residential Care Act 1984, there is currently no regulation of home care. There is no control over the market, and anyone, even if they have a criminal record, is free to set up a home care business and provide services to vulnerable people who need care, living in their own homes, very often on their own and in relative isolation.

People involved in the provision of home care understand and recognise the dangers inherent in the current system. Many have argued and campaigned at length for some form of statutory regulation. It may yet come.

In the meantime, many local authorities have introduced various forms of voluntary registration and accreditation. Most of these schemes are based on the work of the Joint Advisory Group of Domiciliary Care Associations which published *Standards for the Registration for Domiciliary Care* in 1992. This document has been widely circulated and forms the basis of most of the local schemes, including the subsequent London Domiciliary Care Initiative. The recommended minimum standards for registration for domiciliary care are identified below.

There is no obligation on any home care provider to join a voluntary registration, accreditation or 'approved provider' scheme, all of which have been developed by different authorities to compensate for the absence of statutory legislation. However, most, if not all, authorities that have introduced such schemes will only contract for home care services with providers that are on their accredited list.

The process of accreditation that is usually followed is given on page 83. Sample accreditation schemes may be found in the AMA/ACC/ADSS Guidance on Contracting.

If your organisation is already accredited with one local authority, you may find that that accreditation will be recognised and accepted by other authorities introducing a similar accreditation or 'approved provider' scheme. It is clearly a costly and time-consuming exercise to go through the whole process of accreditation with each authority in which you wish to work. This is one of the disadvantages of such voluntary schemes and the lack of any form of national statutory regulation.

The London Domiciliary Care Initiative recognises accreditation between London boroughs. As such schemes become more widespread, it is likely that authorities will recognise accreditation of agencies in neighbouring authorities.

Managers of home care services should keep the local authority purchasers and the members of the Inspection Unit up to date with improvements in the quality of their service and not leave it all to the annual inspection and renewal of accreditation. This updating can be done by sending them copies of any internal newsletters, training courses, brochures, user satisfaction surveys etc, all of which help to promote the image of the organisation and its home care service.

Checklist for registration

REQUIREMENTS	COMPONENTS
Commercial viability	A business plan Financial/professional references Date and number of company registration (if relevant)
'Fit person' (Registered Homes Act 1984)	Owner/manager possesses relevant qualification Personal and professional references Proven, relevant experience References from service users and carers randomly selected from central file

Written information for users	*The range of services available* *Means of access to services, including any process of assessment* *Cost of services* *Procedures, including complaints* *Employment status* *Legal and insurance implications* *Structure of the agency, number of staff and their qualifications* *Contracts/agreements to provide specified services*
Written information for staff	*Employment status* *Legal and insurance implications* *Job description* *Standards to be attained* *Policies (eg on confidentiality)* *Complaints and grievance procedures*
Legal requirements	*Health and Safety at Work etc Act 1974* *Data Protection Act 1984* *Personal Information Act 1989* *Professional liability insurance* *Indemnity insurance* *Requirements of the Nursing Agency register (if relevant)*
Recruitment and selection	*Outline/Detailed personnel policies on:* *Recruitment advertising* *Recruitment interviewing* *Equal opportunities and non-discriminatory practice* *Taking up of references (personal and professional)* *Contracts of employment (where applicable)* *Induction programme*
Assuring quality services	*A mechanism for checking on the standards of services provided* *Service users' views sought* *Quality assurance procedures for the ongoing monitoring of standards* *A standard process for assessing care needs* *A training and development policy for all staff*

Process of accreditation

- Advertising for expressions of interest in the local and national press.
- Explanation of process, forms, etc, at public meetings.
- Application process: provider gives details of services to be provided; policies/procedures; staffing structure, staff recruitment/selection/ training; information on financial viability.
- Interview with provider/proprietor/manager; visit a sample of service users.
- Visit to premises to verify procedures for health and safety, data protection, etc.
- Review and inspection.

THE CONTRACTING PROCESS

There are a number of stages in the contracting process; they are shown in the diagram on the following page and discussed below.

Service specifications

The first stage is the development of service specifications by the pur-chaser. The *Guidance on Contracting for Domiciliary and Day Care Services* recommends that specifications include the following:

- Care principles: broad expectations of the kind of service sought – eg user-centred; reliable; flexible; maintaining independence, dignity, privacy and choice.
- Description of service.
- Priorities for delivery of the service, including eligibility criteria.
- Recruitment and training of staff, including screening.
- General conduct: misconduct rules, gifts, money, etc.
- Confidentiality.
- People at risk: duty and procedure to inform.
- Quality control, including complaints procedure.
- Health and safety.

THE CONTRACTING PROCESS

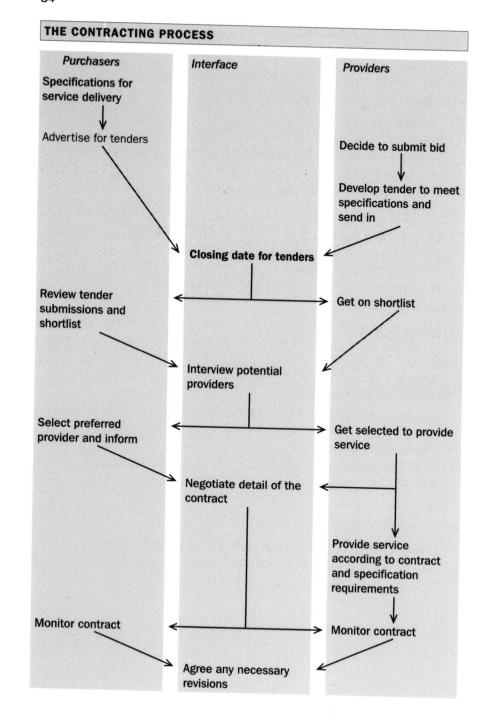

Purchasers

Specifications for service delivery

Advertise for tenders

Review tender submissions and shortlist

Select preferred provider and inform

Monitor contract

Interface

Closing date for tenders

Interview potential providers

Negotiate detail of the contract

Agree any necessary revisions

Providers

Decide to submit bid

Develop tender to meet specifications and send in

Get on shortlist

Get selected to provide service

Provide service according to contract and specification requirements

Monitor contract

- Information to be provided for service users.
- Support to staff working when the office is closed.

Putting the specification out to tender

Invitations to tender for the provision of services may be advertised locally or nationally. If the authority operates an accreditation scheme, voluntary registration or 'approved provider' list, only organisations that are part of the scheme and have already met the authority's criteria for inclusion will generally be invited to submit tenders.

You, as the manager of a service, or others in your organisation will have to decide whether or not you should develop a tender. When an authority invites tenders to provide home care service, they are often seeking four or five provider organisations, not just one. This may influence your decision.

Making a bid

A number of considerations come into this decision. For example:

- What type of contract are they offering – will it give you a degree of security or uncertainty?
- Do you think you have a fair chance of success?
- Has your organisation the capacity, or will it over-stretch your resources?
- Will you need to recruit new staff? Are they available in the marketplace?
- Will your unit price be competitive?
- How badly do you want/need the work?
- Does it fit in with the business plan?

Having decided to proceed, you and your organisation must then ensure that you submit a competitive tender. All the thought and planning that went into developing the business plan should now assist and 'inform' the development of your bid.

NEGOTIATING THE CONTRACT

When your organisation wins the contract, you will need to negotiate its terms and then manage the provision of service according to those terms. It is therefore essential to ensure, as far as you possibly can, that all eventualities are covered by the contract and that you do not unnecessarily or inadvertently place your service at risk. You must make sure that the following issues are covered, either in the contract itself or in an appended document or specification. Failure to include these items in one of these documents is likely to create difficulties for you.

- Emergencies: agree in advance how much additional work should be undertaken to ensure that the person needing care (the service user) is not left alone or vulnerable – eg provide an additional hour of support and then refer back to the care manager. (The policies and procedures of the organisation should include ways to deal with emergencies.)

- Case conferences: costs of attending and travelling time.

- Costs of staff travelling between service users.

- Arrangements for reviewing prices.

- Arrangements for reviewing the needs of the service user.

- Payment for visits where entry is refused (for whatever reason) or the person is not at home.

- Amount of advance notice required for termination of service and/or periods of absence of the service user (hospitalisation, holidays etc).

- Arrangements for additional services provided for the service user if necessary, and how this can trigger re-assessment.

- Protocol and procedures if the local authority requires you to collect the person's financial contribution to the service as part of the payment to your organisation. (Some social services departments are beginning to make use of 'swipe' cards for the payment of services.)

- What happens if the service user does not, or cannot, pay?

- Method and time of payments for service delivery.

- Notice required for visits of purchaser to service user to monitor the contract.

- Rules about subcontracting if you are temporarily unable to provide a service.

Ensuring that all these issues are covered when negotiating the contract will make the task of monitoring it that much simpler.

Monitoring the contract

As manager of the home care service, it will almost certainly be one of your tasks to monitor the contract on a continuing basis to ensure that the service for which you are responsible is meeting all aspects of both the contract and the specification. This is known as *contract compliance*.

It is important not to forget the specification. Many local authorities are putting the detail of the service to be provided into the specification, leaving the contract to cover the strictly legal issues and terms and conditions. You need to ensure that the detail of the specification is met in full.

Its importance can be illustrated by a recent event in one authority when nearly 100 frail people were hospitalised with salmonella poisoning from their Meals on Wheels. The specification – which was very detailed – stated that powdered egg was to be used, but the contractor used fresh egg which resulted in the poisoning. The local authority, which is still responsible even though the service was provided by an external contractor, is being sued; the money will be claimed back from the contractor's insurance.

KEY POINTS

- Most contracts for home care are spot contracts or cost and volume contracts. There are as yet very few block contracts in this area of care.

- There is no national system for regulating the provision of home care that is comparable to the Registered Homes Act 1984.

- Many local authority social services departments have set up their own (voluntary) accreditation or 'approved provider' schemes.

- Most authorities with such schemes will invite only organisations and agencies that are in the scheme to provide home care services on their behalf.

- Weigh up all the factors before making a decision on whether to tender.

- Make sure that all factors are reflected in the contract and the associated specification.

- Monitor the contract to ensure that you comply with all aspects of its specification. To do otherwise could prove costly to your business and to the person receiving care.

6 Managing User-centred Services

This chapter relates to Management standards:

M1 1.1, 1.2, 6.1–6.4, 7.1, 8.1, 9.1–9.3

M2 1.1–1.5, 2.2–2.4, 7.1–7.4, 8.1, 9.1, 9.2, 10.1, 10.2

Managers of home care services have a responsibility to ensure, as far as possible, that the services are provided in a way that places the needs of the person receiving care before the needs of the organisation and of the person providing the care and before the needs of the organisation purchasing the care.

Establishing an operational framework of policies, practices and procedures should help in developing 'person-centred' services, as should the underpinning values when put into practice. Quality assurance systems also support the delivery of services that focus on the needs of the individual person (see Chapter 3).

As the manager responsible, you need to be certain that your staff are delivering the quality and kind of service that the organisation expects. A number of aspects relating to the delivery of 'user-centred' services are explored in this chapter (as well as in Chapters 3 and 4).

If you are ever in doubt about whether the service you manage is user-centred, try putting yourself in the place of the person needing care. Try asking yourself such key questions as:

- Would I like this to happen to me?
- How would I feel?
- How would I like to be treated?

- How important would my rights of privacy, dignity, independence and to take risks be to me?

Once you think you know how you would wish to be treated in similar circumstances, there is no reason why other people should be treated any differently.

Remember that this approach also applies to your staff. They cannot be expected to provide a user-centred service if they do not feel that they are consulted or given any real choice. Employing organisations must practise what they preach if they are to provide a quality service.

ASSESSMENT OF NEED

An assessment of a person's need for home care may be undertaken by the manager of the service itself. For services provided on behalf of the local authority, it may be done by someone responsible for assessing care needs, putting together packages of care to meet the needs and commissioning the provision of services. This process is commonly referred to as 'care management'.

As the manager of home care services, you need to understand the assessment process, even if you are not normally directly responsible yourself for assessment. Module 1 of UNISON's OPAL 2 package for care service managers contains open learning material on the assessment process. There are a number of levels of assessment. The Department of Health's Guidance on Care Management and Assessment identifies six levels from simple through to comprehensive. Managers of care services are likely to be involved only in assessment at the first, or lower, simple levels of need.

An effective assessment of need should:
- Have the person with care needs as its focus.
- Identify what the person is able to do for themselves, as well as identify their care needs.
- Consider the whole person and their environment, not just the presenting problem.

- Take account of what the person needing care is saying – their views and preferences.
- Seek to support and promote the independence of the person.
- Be flexible and creative in the ways identified to meet needs.
- Be outcome orientated in order to achieve the goals identified by the person needing care; eg 'in order to remain in their own home for as long as possible it is necessary to . . .'.

You may find it helpful to obtain an assessment form from your local authority social services department. This will give you an idea what questions are asked. An example of an assessment of need form appears in Appendix 9.

It is not unknown for managers to make their own assessment of need in addition to that undertaken by the care manager or person commissioning the care. Although an understandable precaution, it should not be necessary if the official assessment was done professionally. It can be unsettling and worrying for the person needing care to be asked all the same or similar questions twice. It is contrary to the purpose of developing a user focus.

Health and safety risk assessment

As the manager of home care services, you will be responsible for assessing the health and safety risks associated with providing care to people in their own homes. This assessment must be undertaken before someone is sent into the home to provide care.

If you are providing services on behalf of the local authority, this risk assessment should in theory be undertaken at the time of the assessment of need. In practice, though, this is unlikely to happen and you will have to assume responsibility for assessing the risks for the sake of staff you send into the home. (An example of a manual handling risk assessment form is given in Appendix 2.)

Without going into detail on health and safety – much of which may be found in *CareFully* – the areas to be assessed include the following:

- Safety hazards such as worn carpets, overloaded sockets, trailing flexes.
- Manual handling hazards, including helping people in and out of bed or chairs, moving heavy furniture, lifting heavy objects.
- Health and hygiene hazards such as incontinence, pets, signs of infestation, control of substances hazardous to health (COSHH).

If you identify any particular hazard or hazards that give cause for concern, you should discuss the problem fully with the person who is to receive the care and any personal or family carer if they have one. You should explain that it is a hazard not only to your member of staff but also to themselves, and every possibility should be explored to correct the problem. (See also Chapter 3.)

However, this chapter concerns developing user-centred services, so the need to reduce risks and potential hazards to health and safety has to be balanced with the rights and wishes of the individual person living their own chosen lifestyle within their own home. Their views and wishes concerning the safety of their home must be respected, and they have the right to take calculated risks.

If the hazards are potentially very dangerous, you have the right to refuse to send somebody into the home – but you would only want to do this in extreme circumstances and as a final resort. All other avenues and possibilities should be explored first.

INTRODUCING YOURSELF AND THE SERVICE

Whoever undertakes the assessment of need and the risk assessment, you, as the manager responsible for the service, will still wish to visit the person yourself in order to introduce yourself and the service. This may be combined with the risk assessment if it has not already been carried out. In the initial meeting you will need to:

- Explain who you are and your position in the organisation.
- Introduce the person to the organisation and the care it will provide to meet the assessed needs.

- Provide written information about the organisation, including a contact name and address.
- Establish how the person wishes to be addressed.
- Find out the person's view of their care needs and their wishes and preferences as to when and how the care is provided.
- Clarify the tasks to be undertaken, paying particular attention to personal care tasks and those involving the handling of money.
- Find out if they are likely to require any help with medication and, if so, indicate the limits of the help the home carer can provide.
- Establish how the home carer is to gain entry to the home. If the carer is to have her or his own key, it should be numbered or coded rather than labelled with the address.
- Warn the service user to allow only home care staff with the appropriate identification into their home – even if they are known personally to them. Ex-employees have been known to return and steal from their previous service users.
- Reassure the person that every effort will be made to provide the care in the way they wish.
- Clarify the organisation's policies and practices that directly affect the provision of care – this should include the underpinning values of the organisation.
- Begin to establish the kind of person they would like to provide their care.
- Inform the person about the complaints procedure and leave written information.
- Emphasise that the home carer is present to provide support and assistance to enable them to stay in their own home and maintain a degree of independence. Reassure them that the carer is not there to take over their life.

If the person needing care is paying privately for the care, you will also need to agree with them your organisation's terms and conditions for providing the care, including:

- home insurance cover;
- cancellation at short notice;
- termination of the contract.

The information gained at this initial meeting should be confirmed in writing with the person concerned and passed on to the home carer in due course.

A copy of an Individual Service Contract (ISC) will be found in the *Guidance on Contracting for Domiciliary and Day Care*. A signed copy of this – or a similar contract – should be left with a copy of your brochure and details of the complaints procedure in the person's home for future reference and as a reminder about what has been agreed.

Matching the home carer to the person needing care

It is becoming increasingly common, wherever possible, to give the person receiving care a choice in the person who provides the care. Much of the care will include undertaking some personal and therefore intimate tasks and it is essential that the person feels relaxed and comfortable with their home carer.

Staff are your front-line ambassadors and it is important to match skills, knowledge and personal attributes with the needs and preferences of the person needing care. It is particularly important to make every effort to match the religious and cultural needs of people from ethnic communities with those of their carer. If this is not possible – because there is a shortage of home carers from the relevant ethnic community – no one from another culture should be expected to provide care without appropriate training and acquiring the necessary skills and knowledge.

To place a home carer without this training with a person from an ethnic community is unfair to the home carer and could be considered an insult to the person needing care and their culture or religion. It would also undermine the application of the organisation's values.

At the same time, however, you have a responsibility to protect your staff from discrimination and harassment. You will need to decide the action you will take if, for example:

- a person needing care discriminates against the home carer on the basis of their colour, race, gender or sexual orientation, or taunts and provokes them when they are doing their job;
- a man continually harasses the female carer, either physically or verbally.

You have the right and the responsibility to take the home carer away from an unacceptable work environment, even if this leaves the person temporarily without care. In the case of the man, you could try providing two carers – which would be expensive – or recruit a male home carer. The dilemma is that you should also be sensitive to the older person's prejudices. These will be deep-seated, and come from their past when the world was very different.

THE CARE PLAN

If the needs of the person receiving care have been assessed by the social services department, there should be a care plan that identifies the care needs, how they are being met and the required outcomes. It is good practice for a copy of the care plan to be left with the person to whom it refers; you and the home carer should have access to the plan in order to make sure that you are meeting the identified needs and to co-ordinate the provision of care with others (eg Meals on Wheels, day care or visits from the district nurse).

Even when you are providing care privately or through a voluntary organisation, and the local social services department is not involved, it is still good practice to develop your own care plan to ensure that the needs are met. An example of a care plan is given in Appendix 10.

The care plan should identify the tasks undertaken by the home carer. However, in developing user-centred services, it is also good practice to encourage home carers to ask the people they are caring for what they want done. This enables them to make choices about their care needs and allows for other needs, which may not be part of the care plan, to be met as well.

Obviously there has to be a balance, and meeting the needs outlined in the care plan must take priority. Nevertheless, some flexibility should be possible. If yours is a private organisation providing care on behalf of the local authority, the person receiving care may ask for extra services (eg meals prepared on days not scheduled in the care plan), and offer to pay for them privately.

It is sensible in these circumstances to clear this first with the social services department as the principal contractor. They will need to be reassured that, on the one hand, the person is not being encouraged to pay for services they don't need and, on the other, the request does not indicate a need for a review.

Review of care need

There should be regular review of need every six or twelve months. The date of the review should be written into the care plan. However, it is well known that, when there is pressure on time and the workload is heavy, review of need is the first casualty: it is not considered to be a high-priority activity. People receiving home care have been known to go for a number of years without having a review – at least they are receiving a service and the assumption is that, if there is a significant change in the condition of the person, the home carer will tell the line manager and trigger a review of the care.

This issue of review of need has long been a problem. It is now exacerbated in social service departments in which responsibility for review lies with the care manager as part of the commissioning function rather than with the manager providing the service.

As a manager of the home care service, you have a double responsibility: to monitor the services being provided to make sure that they meet the needs identified; and to trigger review if circumstances change or if the health and abilities of the person being cared for deteriorate. Your staff must know the circumstances in which they should indicate to you, as the manager, that they think a review is required (see *CareFully*).

It might be helpful at the beginning to agree with the service user the action they wish you to take if their condition worsens. Whom would they like you to contact – the members of their family, their GP, neighbours or someone else? You will, of course, need to inform the social services department to trigger a review. This agreement should be recorded in the Individual Service Contract which, along with the care plan, should be left in the person's home.

Collaboration with other agencies

If there are several or complex care needs, the package of care is likely to be provided by a number of agencies, each supplying a different service (eg health services, Meals on Wheels, day care). In these circumstances, every effort should be made to co-ordinate the days and times on which services are provided. This will ensure that people do not all turn up at once, confusing or inconveniencing the person needing care.

One way to help in this situation is to keep a diary or record in the person's home which shows when people should be coming and also allows each agency to record, for everyone to see, what has happened. Such a diary can be particularly important in the administration of medication when family carers, home carers and trained health care staff can record what medication has been taken. It also helps when handling the service user's money.

If intensive home care is required, more than one agency may be involved in providing the care; for example, local authority in-house services during the week and private agencies at weekends. A diary helps the transfer of responsibility from one agency to another and brings everyone up to date with what has happened in their absence. It also helps to ensure continuity of care.

Complaints and compliments

At your first visit to the person needing care, you should have left a brochure or leaflet giving information about your organisation, including a clear statement of the complaints policy and procedure. Developing a user-centred service includes encouraging people to say if they are not happy with the service they receive, and encouraging them to complain.

This is very important in home care because most people receiving care are very reluctant to complain. The vast majority are pleased and grateful to have the service, and are afraid that it might be withdrawn. This can apply even if people are receiving the service privately and paying for it themselves.

Perhaps the word 'complaint' is the barrier. Other words may help: for example, you can explain that you need to know if something is not right, so that you can improve the standard of the service. If you don't know, because you have not been told, you cannot do anything about it.

It may also help if you emphasise equally that you also need to know when things are done well and to receive the compliments as well as the complaints. These should then be passed on to the staff concerned, to provide a more balanced approach instead of continually focusing on the negative aspects of the service.

Regular surveys of people receiving care are one way of ensuring that the service you are providing is meeting their needs. It may be quite a simple form that the home carer can leave in the home on one visit and pick up – hopefully completed – the next. Although there is a tendency for such forms to become a measure of the 'feel good' factor, they can, nevertheless, give you a reasonable idea of how your service is perceived by the people who are receiving it. Such surveys will, however, rarely reveal the true complaints and you will still need to promote your full complaints procedure.

KEY POINTS

- Develop a user-centred service – think how you would feel if you were receiving home care.

- Introduce yourself to each new person receiving your service and establish basic details (eg what they prefer to be called). Leave with them all the details of your service and contact points.

- Try to give the person a choice of who becomes their home carer. Match people with their home carer.

- Undertake an assessment of risk in the home, as required by law.

- Make sure that each person has their own care plan and that the home carer is aware of their contribution to achieving the required outcome.

- Trigger a review of need if the health or physical condition of the person deteriorates.

- Liaise with people from other agencies and organisations (eg health) who may also be providing care, to ensure that visits are co-ordinated.

- Encourage people to let you know when they are pleased with the service they receive, as well as when they think it might be improved. Try to remove the barrier to complaining and make it an acceptable process.

7 Managing Yourself

This chapter relates to Management standards:

M1 5,3

M2 6.3, 6.4

IDENTIFYING YOUR PERSONAL STRENGTHS AND WEAKNESSES

You need to be able to manage yourself if you are going to manage others effectively. The four areas in the checklist below are a good starting point. Go through the checklist and decide whether each item represents a personal strength or a weakness (place a tick or cross in the relevant column).

Managing self checklist

UNITS	STRENGTH	WEAKNESS
A Managing others to optimise results		
1 Showing sensitivity to the needs of others	————	————
2 Relating to others	————	————
3 Obtaining the commitment of others	————	————
4 Presenting oneself positively to others	————	————

B Planning to optimise results

1 Showing concern for excellence   _____ _____

2 Setting and prioritising objectives   _____ _____

3 Monitoring and responding to actual against
planned activities   _____ _____

C Taking responsibility for self

1 Showing self-confidence and personal drive   _____ _____

2 Managing personal emotions   _____ _____

3 Managing personal learning and development   _____ _____

D Managing problem solving

1 Collecting and organising information   _____ _____

2 Identifying and applying concepts   _____ _____

3 Taking decisions   _____ _____

You will then need to decide what action to take to improve your skills in the areas you have indicated are weaknesses. You may get some ideas from the section on personal development, later in this chapter. Why are these areas important? Consider the reasons listed below.

Managing others to optimise results will:

- help staff feel valued, supported and able to carry out their work, which will encourage them to stay with your organisation;
- build an effective team that will ensure quality;
- build effective relationships with social services, commissioners of services, inspection and quality units etc;
- ensure the confidence of people receiving care, commissioners, etc in the quality and reliability of the service that will be delivered.

Planning to optimise results will help you to:

- ensure quality in the staff employed and the service provided;
- prioritise and manage time effectively to ensure that the service runs smoothly and that the stress levels of staff and yourself are manageable;
- ensure that your business plan is achievable;
- take steps to remedy any change that will affect your level of service and cash flow.

Taking responsibility for self will help you to:

- inspire staff, the people receiving care and the social services to have confidence in your service;
- set an example to staff;
- manage stress to ensure that your health, and therefore the health of the organisation, does not suffer;
- evaluate situations and relationships, and learn from them.

Managing problem solving helps you ensure that accurate information is readily accessible so as to make informed decisions about:

- staff rotas;
- time sheets;
- complaints from people receiving care, their carers or the purchasers of services;
- accidents;
- emergencies;
- finance and budgets;
- training of staff;
- levels of stress and sickness;
- grievances and staff discipline;
- records of services provided to people.

MAKING EFFECTIVE USE OF TIME

All managers complain about not having enough time to complete their work, but do we use the time available to us effectively?

Complete the exercise on page 102. In the first column list all the main activities you undertake in a normal week. In the second column note an estimate of the number of hours you spend on each activity in the week. In the third column rank each activity as to its importance in enabling you to manage the delivery of high quality home care services, on a scale of 1–5: 1 = not at all important; 2 = not important; 3 = neither important nor unimportant; 4 = important; 5 = very important.

MAKING EFFECTIVE USE OF TIME

Activity	Hours	Priority	Action

Are you making the most effective use of the time that is available? Are you spending most of your time on high priority activities or is a lot of time devoted to activities that you consider to be of low priority?

In the fourth column indicate the activities where you can and should take action to reduce the amount of time spent to free you to do more important work.

Consider your job description:

- Does it reflect your current role accurately or does it need updating?
- Does it reflect managing the provision of care services on a business-like basis?
- Does it include the contracting process?
- Does it take account of the introduction of NVQs and your possible involvement in assessing practice?

Many managers claim they do not have the time to assess practice. This is usually because they are adding assessment to their previous role and job description, instead of looking at how the management task is changing and making assessment an integral part of the work.

Do you need to reappraise your management role and amend or even rewrite your job description?

UNDERPINNING VALUES

Chapter 3 discussed the importance of each home care organisation having a clear set of values to underpin the provision of its services. These values should be explicit, developed in conjunction with staff and shared with the people receiving care and the commissioners or purchasers of care. As the manager, you must lead by example.

The following exercise is based on the value base unit of the Care Awards: Unit 0 'Promote equality for all individuals'. For each of the five areas, list what you *already do* in the organisation. Then add what further action you could take to promote equality. Share this with staff and see whether it can be put into practice. Space is left in the form for you to insert a sixth value for your agency or organisation.

104

UNDERPINNING VALUE BASE

0.a Promote anti-discriminatory practice

Action already taken

Action could take

0.b Maintain the confidentiality of information

Action already taken

Action could take

0.c Promote and support individual rights and choice within service delivery

Action already taken

Action could take

0.d Acknowledge individuals' personal beliefs and identity

Action already taken

Action could take

0.e Support individuals through effective communication

Action already taken

Action could take

Action already taken

Action could take

PERSONAL DEVELOPMENT NEEDS

As you have read through this book, you may have identified some areas in which you have further development needs. You need to build on your strengths and plan your own training and development to turn your weaknesses into strengths. There are a number of different ways this might be done. Some of them are listed here. Contact addresses may be found in the Useful Addresses section.

- Undertake a care management qualification such as the Local Government Management Board (LGMB) Diploma in the Management of Care Services covering the NVQ 4/level 1 Management standards (see next section) or a generic management qualification such as the Certificate or Diploma in Management Studies.
- Assemble your management portfolio to provide evidence for the NVQ level 4 or 5 Management qualification (see next section).
- Contact your local Training and Enterprise Council and your local Enterprise Agency (see *Yellow Pages*).
- Find out what local colleges have to offer.
- Join one or more of the professional associations – BADCO, UKHCA, SCA (see Useful Addresses).
- Network with other providers for support and access to training and development opportunities.
- See what assistance your local social services department can offer.

NVQ Management standards

You will undoubtedly be familiar with the NVQ level 2 and 3 Care standards but probably less familiar with the Management standards. These were developed by the Management Charter Initiative, in parallel with the work being undertaken on developing the NVQ standards, and have been adopted by the National Council for Vocational Qualifications. The relation between the Care standards and the Management standards is:

National Vocational Qualifications (NVQs)

Care awards	*Management standards*
Level 2	
Level 3	
Level 4	Level 4 *First line management*
	Level 5 *Middle management*
	Level 5 *Senior management*

It should only be a short while before it becomes possible to progress through the Care awards into the Management standards. At present (1996), NVQs do not go beyond level 5, hence two level 5 management qualifications

Details of the first line and middle management standards, to which the content of this book relates, are given in Appendix 1. The structure is similar to that for the Care awards:

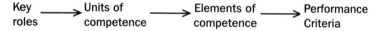

Key ⟶ Units of ⟶ Elements of ⟶ Performance
roles   competence   competence   Criteria

The Diploma in the Management of Care Services offered by the LGMB covers all the level 4 Management standards and relates them to social care. The Diploma also incorporates the 0 unit – the value base of the care sector.

UNISON published the OPAL 2 package – Open and Assisted Learning for Managers of Care Services – in early 1996. This is related to the first line management standards and provides useful background material for a range of training activities as well as an introduction to the LGMB Diploma.

The Department of Health and the NHS Training Executive have produced an open learning package, Health and Social Services Management, which incorporates the middle management standards.

You can also obtain your NVQ Management qualification by the system of APEL – accreditation of prior experience and learning. For this you assemble a portfolio of evidence of competence in practice in each of the units and elements, which is assessed. Further information may be obtained from the Management Charter Initiative or from Insight Consultants (see Useful Addresses).

A useful exercise would be for you to make an audit of your management competence. Decide whether you are a first line or a middle manager and then complete the appropriate part of the following checklist – which is directly related to the two levels of management qualification. Identifying the areas in which you are already competent and noting those where you need to improve will enable you to plan your future development programme.

FIRST LINE MANAGEMENT STANDARDS – NVQ 4

Place a tick in the box that most closely describes your competence in relation to that activity.

I do this and consider that I:

	am competent	need more competence	lack competence	I do not do this
Manage operations				
1 Maintain and improve service and product operations				
1.1 Maintain operations to meet quality standards	☐	☐	☐	☐
1.2 Create and maintain the necessary conditions for productive work	☐	☐	☐	☐
2 Contribute to the implementation of change in services, products and systems				
2.1 Contribute to the evaluation of proposed changes to services, products and systems	☐	☐	☐	☐
2.2 Implement and evaluate changes to services, products and systems	☐	☐	☐	☐
Manage finance				
3 Recommend, monitor and control the use of resources				
3.1 Make recommendations for expenditure	☐	☐	☐	☐

	I do this and consider that I:			
	am competent	*need more competence*	*lack competence*	**I do not do this**
3.2 Monitor and control the use of resources	☐	☐	☐	☐
Manage people				
4 Contribute to the recruitment and selection of personnel				
4.1 Define future personnel requirements	☐	☐	☐	☐
4.2 Contribute to the assessment and selection of candidates against team and organisational requirements	☐	☐	☐	☐
5 Develop teams, individuals and self to enhance performance				
5.1 Develop and improve teams through planning and activities	☐	☐	☐	☐
5.2 Identify, review and improve development activities for individuals	☐	☐	☐	☐
5.3 Develop oneself within the job role	☐	☐	☐	☐
6 Plan, allocate and evaluate work carried out by teams, individuals and self				
6.1 Set and update work objectives for teams and individuals	☐	☐	☐	☐
6.2 Plan activities and determine work methods to achieve objectives	☐	☐	☐	☐
6.3 Allocate work and evaluate teams, individuals and self against objectives	☐	☐	☐	☐
6.4 Provide feedback to teams and individuals on their performance	☐	☐	☐	☐
7 Create, maintain and enhance effective working relationships				
7.1 Establish and maintain the trust and support of one's subordinates	☐	☐	☐	☐

| | **I do this and consider that I:** | | | |
	am competent	need more competence	lack competence	I do not do this
7.2 Establish and maintain the trust and support of one's immediate manager	☐	☐	☐	☐
7.3 Establish and maintain relationships with colleagues	☐	☐	☐	☐
7.4 Identify and minimise interpersonal conflict	☐	☐	☐	☐
7.5 Implement disciplinary and grievance procedures	☐	☐	☐	☐
7.6 Counsel staff	☐	☐	☐	☐

Manage information

8 Seek, evaluate and organise information for action

8.1 Obtain and evaluate information to aid decision making	☐	☐	☐	☐
8.2 Record and store information	☐	☐	☐	☐

9 Exchange information to solve problems and make decisions

9.1 Lead meetings and group discussions to solve problems and make decisions	☐	☐	☐	☐
9.2 Contribute to discussions to solve problems and make decisions	☐	☐	☐	☐
9.3 Advise and inform others	☐	☐	☐	☐

MIDDLE MANAGEMENT STANDARDS – NVQ 5

Place a tick in the box that most closely describes your competence in relation to that activity.

	I do this and consider that I:			
	am competent	*need more competence*	*lack competence*	**I do not do this**
Manage operations				
1 Initiate and implement change and improvements in products and services				
1.1 Identify opportunities for improvements in services, products and systems	☐	☐	☐	☐
1.2 Evaluate proposed changes for benefits and disadvantages	☐	☐	☐	☐
1.3 Negotiate and agree the introduction of change	☐	☐	☐	☐
1.4 Implement and evaluate changes to services, products and systems	☐	☐	☐	☐
1.5 Introduce, develop and evaluate quality assurance systems	☐	☐	☐	☐
2 Monitor, maintain and improve service and product delivery				
2.1 Establish and maintain the supply of resources into the organisation/ department	☐	☐	☐	☐
2.2 Establish and agree customer requirements	☐	☐	☐	☐
2.3 Maintain and improve operations against quality and functional specifications	☐	☐	☐	☐
2.4 Create and maintain the necessary conditions for productive work	☐	☐	☐	☐

		I do this and consider that I:			
		am competent	*need more competence*	*lack competence*	**I do not do this**
Manage finance					
3	Monitor and control the use of resources				
3.1	Control costs and enhance value	☐	☐	☐	☐
3.2	Monitor and control activities against budgets	☐	☐	☐	☐
4	Secure effective resource allocation for activities and projects				
4.1	Justify proposals for expenditure on projects	☐	☐	☐	☐
4.2	Negotiate and agree budgets	☐	☐	☐	☐
Manage people					
5	Recruit and select personnel				
5.1	Define future personnel requirements	☐	☐	☐	☐
5.2	Determine specifications to secure quality people	☐	☐	☐	☐
5.3	Assess and select candidates against team and organisational requirements	☐	☐	☐	☐
6	Develop teams, individuals and self to enhance performance				
6.1	Develop and improve teams through planning and activities	☐	☐	☐	☐
6.2	Identify, review and improve development activities for individuals	☐	☐	☐	☐
6.3	Develop oneself within the job role	☐	☐	☐	☐
6.4	Evaluate and improve the development processes used	☐	☐	☐	☐
7	Plan, allocate and evaluate work carried out by teams, individuals and self				
7.1	Set and update work objectives for teams and individuals	☐	☐	☐	☐

	I do this and consider that I:			
	am competent	*need more competence*	*lack competence*	**I do not do this**
7.2 Plan activities and determine work methods to achieve objectives	☐	☐	☐	☐
7.3 Allocate work and evaluate teams, individuals and self against objectives	☐	☐	☐	☐
7.4 Provide feedback to teams and individuals on their performance	☐	☐	☐	☐
8 Create, maintain and enhance effective working relationships	☐	☐	☐	☐
8.1 Establish and maintain the trust and support of one's subordinates	☐	☐	☐	☐
8.2 Establish and maintain the trust and support of one's manager	☐	☐	☐	☐
8.3 Establish and maintain relationships with colleagues	☐	☐	☐	☐
8.4 Identify and minimise interpersonal conflict	☐	☐	☐	☐
8.5 Implement disciplinary and grievance procedures	☐	☐	☐	☐
8.6 Counsel staff	☐	☐	☐	☐
Manage information				
9 Seek, evaluate and organise information for action				
9.1 Obtain and evaluate information to aid decision making	☐	☐	☐	☐
9.2 Forecast trends and developments which affect objectives	☐	☐	☐	☐
9.3 Record and store information	☐	☐	☐	☐
10 Exchange information to solve problems and make decisions				
10.1 Lead meetings and group discussions to solve problems and make decisions	☐	☐	☐	☐
10.2 Contribute to discussions to solve problems and make decisions	☐	☐	☐	☐
10.3 Advise and inform others	☐	☐	☐	☐

The Appendices

Appendix 1
NVQ Management standards

Appendix 2
Example of manual handling risk assessment form

Appendix 3
Example of an accident record form

Appendix 4
Example of a job description

Appendix 5
Example of a person specification

Appendix 6
Sample interview questions: home care assistant

Appendix 7
Example of a conditions of service

Appendix 8
Example of a disciplinary procedure

Appendix 9
Example of assessment of need form

Appendix 10
Example of a care plan

Appendix 1

NVQ MANAGEMENT STANDARDS

OVERVIEW OF THE M1 FIRST LINE MANAGEMENT STANDARDS

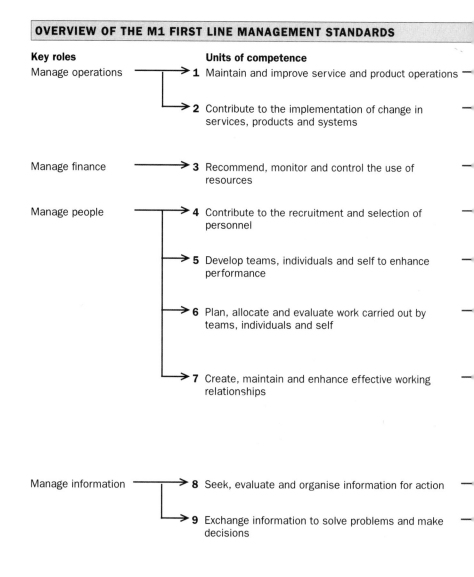

Key roles

Units of competence

Manage operations → **1** Maintain and improve service and product operations —

→ **2** Contribute to the implementation of change in services, products and systems —

Manage finance → **3** Recommend, monitor and control the use of resources —

Manage people → **4** Contribute to the recruitment and selection of personnel —

→ **5** Develop teams, individuals and self to enhance performance —

→ **6** Plan, allocate and evaluate work carried out by teams, individuals and self —

→ **7** Create, maintain and enhance effective working relationships —

Manage information → **8** Seek, evaluate and organise information for action —

→ **9** Exchange information to solve problems and make decisions —

Elements of competence

→ **1.1** Maintain operations to meet quality standards
1.2 Create and maintain the necessary conditions for productive work

→ **2.1** Contribute to the evaluation of proposed changes to services, products and systems
2.2 Implement and evaluate changes to services, products and systems

→ **3.1** Make recommendations for expenditure
3.2 Monitor and control the use of resources

→ **4.1** Define future personnel requirements
4.2 Contribute to the assessment and selection of candidates against team and organisational requirements

→ **5.1** Develop and improve teams through planning and activities
5.2 Identify, review and improve development activities for individuals
5.3 Develop oneself within the job role

→ **6.1** Set and update work objectives for teams and individuals
6.2 Plan activities and determine work methods to achieve objectives
6.3 Allocate work and evaluate teams, individuals and self against objectives
6.4 Provide feedback to teams and individuals on their performance

→ **7.1** Establish and maintain the trust and support of one's subordinates
7.2 Establish and maintain the trust and support of one's immediate manager
7.3 Establish and maintain relationships with colleagues
7.4 Identify and minimise interpersonal conflict
7.5 Implement disciplinary and grievance procedures
7.6 Counsel staff

→ **8.1** Obtain and evaluate information to aid decision making
8.2 Record and store information

→ **9.1** Lead meetings and group discussions to solve problems and make decisions
9.2 Contribute to discussions to solve problems and make decisions
9.3 Advise and inform others

OVERVIEW OF THE M2 MIDDLE MANAGEMENT STANDARDS

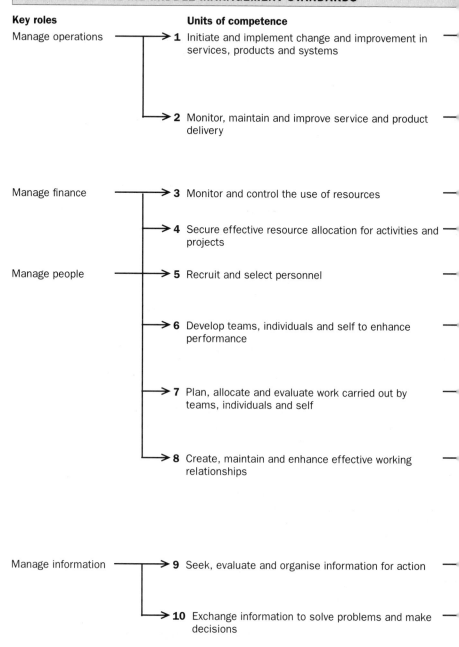

Key roles

Units of competence

Manage operations

1 Initiate and implement change and improvement in services, products and systems

2 Monitor, maintain and improve service and product delivery

Manage finance

3 Monitor and control the use of resources

4 Secure effective resource allocation for activities and projects

Manage people

5 Recruit and select personnel

6 Develop teams, individuals and self to enhance performance

7 Plan, allocate and evaluate work carried out by teams, individuals and self

8 Create, maintain and enhance effective working relationships

Manage information

9 Seek, evaluate and organise information for action

10 Exchange information to solve problems and make decisions

Elements of competence

1.1 Identify opportunities for improvement in services, products and systems
1.2 Evaluate proposed changes for benefits and disadvantages
1.3 Negotiate and agree the introduction of change
1.4 Implement and evaluate changes to services, products and systems
1.5 Introduce, develop and evaluate quality assurance systems

2.1 Establish and maintain the supply of resources into the organisation/department
2.2 Establish and agree customer requirements
2.3 Maintain and improve operations against quality and functional specifications
2.4 Create and maintain the necessary conditions for productive work activity

3.1 Control costs and enhance value
3.2 Monitor and control activities against budgets

4.1 Justify proposals for expenditure on projects
4.2 Negotiate and agree budgets

5.1 Define future personnel requirements
5.2 Determine specifications to secure quality people
5.3 Assess and select candidates against team and organisational requirements

6.1 Develop and improve teams through planning and activities
6.2 Identify, review and improve development activities for individuals
6.3 Develop oneself within the job role
6.4 Evaluate and improve the development processes used

7.1 Set and update work objectives for teams and individuals
7.2 Plan activities and determine work methods to achieve objectives
7.3 Allocate work and evaluate teams, individuals and self against objectives
7.4 Provide feedback to teams and individuals on their performance

8.1 Establish and maintain the trust and support of one's subordinates
8.2 Establish and maintain the trust and support of one's immediate manager
8.3 Establish and maintain relationships with colleagues
8.4 Identify and minimise interpersonal conflict
8.5 Implement disciplinary and grievance procedures
8.6 Counsel staff

9.1 Obtain and evaluate information to aid decision making
9.2 Forecast trends and developments which affect objectives
9.3 Record and store information

10.1 Lead meetings and group discussions to solve problems and make decisions
10.2 Contribute to discussions to solve problems and make decisions
10.3 Advise and inform others

Appendix 2

EXAMPLE OF MANUAL HANDLING RISK ASSESSMENT FORM

The purpose of this assessment is to reduce the risk of manual handling injuries to staff members.

Unit/Team/Locality

Client address

Assessor

Client name

Date of assessment (if applicable)

SUBJECT OF REPORT (tick appropriate box)

Some examples of operations are listed; please tick if appropriate

- ☐ Helping client get out of bed
- ☐ Helping client get out of chair
- ☐ Assisting to stand
- ☐ Toileting
- ☐ Bathing and showering
- ☐ Boarding and alighting from vehicles
- ☐ Transfer/move objects from one height to another

- ☐ Helping client move in bed
- ☐ Putting client to bed
- ☐ Dressing/undressing
- ☐ Washing
- ☐ Carrying object over distance
- ☐ Transfer/move object at level height
- ☐ Transporting wheelchairs

Or specify any other

Statement of policy

When is it not possible to avoid the need for manual handling, specialist lifting equipment will be used to lift either loads or clients, and staff should be trained in the safe use of equipment. Where the use of lifting equipment is not reasonably practicable, other improvements should be explored (eg changes to the environment).

A RISK AVOIDANCE/ELIMINATION

1 Can the operation be avoided? YES/NO
  If 'Yes', the assessment need go no further

2 Do you consider that suitable lifting aids or mechanical YES/NO
  means could be provided to assist in the task?
  If 'No', complete risk assessment.

3 If 'Yes', do you believe that the use of mechanical means or lifting YES/NO
  aids will reduce the manual handling risk to an acceptable level?
  If there is any doubt, answer 'No'.

  IF 'YES', COMPLETE RISK REDUCTION ACTION PLAN

  IF 'NO', COMPLETE RISK ASSESSMENT

B ASSESSMENT CHECKLIST FOR PEOPLE LIFTING PEOPLE

Consider the operation and complete the following by circling the scores as it applies to the operation.

The task

0 No or minimal assistance

5 Twisting/stooping/reaching

3 Assisting over long distances

5 Prolonged physical effort

The client

0 Fully mobile

3 Walks with aids/carer

5 Stands but unable to walk

5 Confused/Dementia/Irrational behaviour/Apprehensive/Anxious

0 Well motivated

5 Unstable gait/unco-ordinated

5 Unable to assist/dead weight

Other risk factors

5 Spinal injury

5 Orthopaedic conditions

5 Prone to falls

5 Tall/Large frame/Substantial size or weight

5 Motor/sensory deficit

5 Heavy sedation

5 Pain

The working environment

0 Spacious, well designed

5 Poor lighting

5 Space limitations that prevent good posture

5 Variations in levels (eg steps, stairs)

3 Weather problems (eg wind, rain, snow)

5 Low bed/low chair

5 Uneven/slippery floor surfaces

5 Other (*please state*)

Individual capability

3 Requires a person of unusual strength/height

5 Creates a hazard to workers who may have a health problem or a medical condition (including pregnancy)

An employee is obliged to advise the employer of any condition that is likely to put him or her at a greater risk of injury (eg pregnancy, recent surgical operations and any relevant medical history).

NB: sufficient rest and recovery periods should be provided for staff.

score from checklist

C LEVEL OF RISK

Taking into account all factors identified above as contributing to the likelihood of the staff member doing this operation being injured, the risk of injury from this operation is:

    Low   10
    Medium   11–20
    High   21+

The higher the risk, the greater remedial action that must be taken to reduce the eventual risk to low or insignificant.

D RISK REDUCTION ACTION PLAN

CONSIDER: can services/equipment be brought to the client rather than take the client to services/equipment?

To reduce the risk of injury to members of staff, the following action will be taken (please tick):

☐ Use of equipment: eg Multiglide, mattress elevator, bath seat, commode, transfer sling, trolley. Please specify:

☐ Re-position furniture
☐ Use team approach – two staff members working together
☐ Refer to OT for equipment evaluation: eg handrails/grabrails, non-slip treads
☐ Specify other risk reduction steps to be taken:

Review staff training (please specify)

Don't forget to update client's care plan and inform staff members of the outcomes from the risk assessment.

Completion date for action:

Assessor's signature:

Date:

This assessment will be reviewed in

B(1) ASSESSMENT CHECKLIST FOR PEOPLE LIFTING INANIMATE OBJECTS

Consider the operation and complete the following by circling the scores as it applies to the operation.

The tasks – do they involve:

3 Carrying over long distances

3 Exclusive pushing or pulling

3 Frequent/prolonged physical effort

3 Insufficient rest or recovery periods

3 Unpredictable movement of loads

3 Assisting over long distances

5 Twisting/stooping/reaching

5 Holding loads away from trunk

The loads – are they:

3 Intrinsically harmful (eg sharp/hot)

5 Heavy

3 Bulky/unwieldy/difficult to grasp

5 Unstable/unpredictable

The working environment – is/are there:

5 Poor lighting

5 Space limitations that prevent
good posture

5 Variations in levels (eg steps, stairs)

5 Weather problems (eg wind, rain,
snow)

5 Uneven/slippery floor surfaces

5 Other (*please state*)

[ ]

Individual capability – does the job:

3 Require a person of unusual
strength/height

5 Create a hazard to workers who may
have a health problem or a medical
condition (including pregnancy)

3 Require special training or information

An employee is obliged to advise the employer of any condition that is likely to put
him or her at a greater risk of injury (eg pregnancy, recent surgical operations and
any relevant medical history).

NB: sufficient rest and recovery periods should be provided for staff.

Total score from checklist [ ]

C(1)LEVEL OF RISK

Taking into account all factors identified above as contributing to the likelihood of
the staff member doing this operation being injured, the risk of injury from this
operation is:

Low   10

Medium   11–20

High   21+

The higher the risk, the greater remedial action that must be taken to reduce the
eventual risk to low or insignificant.

D(1)RISK REDUCTION ACTION PLAN

To reduce the risk of injury to members of staff, the following action will be taken (please tick):

☐ Use of equipment: eg sack truck, trolley

☐ Reduce size of load/smaller quantities ordered

☐ Re-position furniture

☐ Use team approach – two staff members working together

☐ Refer to Safety Adviser for assistance

☐ Specify other risk reduction steps to be taken:

Review staff training (please specify)

Completion date for action:

Assessor's signature: Date:

This assessment will be reviewed in

Reproduced by courtesy of Berkshire County Council

Appendix 3

EXAMPLE OF AN ACCIDENT RECORD FORM

BACKGROUND DETAILS

Employing department

Accident first reported to (name)

Establishment and Department

Date reported

Time reported

SUBJECT OF REPORT (tick appropriate box)

☐ For non-employee,minor injury

☐ 3 days' absence or less (staff only)*

☐ Over 3 days' absence (staff only)*

☐ Specified major injury/condition*
(include hospitalisation of more than
24 hours)

☐ Fatality*

☐ County council employee

☐ Youth trainee

☐ Student/pupil (Education Department)

☐ Client/resident (Social Services)

☐ Other person (describe)

* Reportable by designated management to Health and Safety Executive in accordance
with departmental instructions.

DETAILS OF INJURED PERSON – STAFF ONLY (see over for non-staff)

Surname

Division/section of department

Forenames

Place of work/establishment

Home address

Job title

Date of birth

Sex M/F

Age at date of accident

Lost time as a result of accident? Yes/No

Number of days lost

DETAILS OF ACCIDENT
To be completed for county council employees only

Date of accident

| DAY | MONTH | YEAR |

Part of body affected

Time of accident am/pm

Nature of injury

Address or location of accident

Full account of the circumstances leading to the accident: what was the injured person doing? who else was involved? what equipment or materials were involved? how did the accident happen? (Continue on a separate sheet if necessary.)

Precise place (eg kitchen, workshop, office, stairs)

To be completed for persons *not* employed by the county council

Date of accident

DAY	MONTH	YEAR

Part of body affected

Time of accident am/pm

Nature of injury

Address or location of accident

Full account of the circumstances leading to the accident: what was the injured person doing? who else was involved? what equipment or materials were involved? how did the accident happen? (Continue on a separate sheet if necessary.)

Precise place (eg classroom, playing field, road

Name of any witness

To the best of my knowledge, the particulars stated above constitute a true record of the circumstances relating to the accident.

Signed

Designation

Date

Department

Place of work

Observations of manager in charge and proposed action to avoid recurrence:

Signed

Designation

Date

Information contained in this form is personal data which will be held in a computer and is therefore subject to the Data Protection Act 1984.

Reproduced by courtesy of Berkshire County Council

Appendix 4

EXAMPLE OF A JOB DESCRIPTION

Post title: Home care assistant

Grade:

Responsible to: Home Care Manager

The care provided by a home care assistant is what would normally be given by members of the family and does not include tasks that would normally be undertaken by a trained nurse.

The following list illustrates the types of duties that a home care assistant may be asked to undertake. At all times, a home care assistant must comply with the organisation's guidelines and policies.

- To help people with getting up in the morning, washing/bathing and dressing; helping with undressing and getting to bed in the evening.
- To make meals, drinks and supper-time snacks when necessary.
- To provide assistance with toileting and with changing clothes and/or bedding where necessary; to empty and cleanse commodes, and wash and iron clothes and bed linen (which may include laundry soiled by incontinence) when necessary.
- To provide assistance with other tasks of daily living that the person cannot manage, which may include cleaning, shopping, collecting pension and paying bills.
- Record information on a care sheet when necessary.
- To report to the Home Care Manager any significant changes in the health or social circumstances of the individual.

- To encourage people towards a degree of independence and activity appropriate to their abilities.

- Within an agreed plan and in consultation with the Home Care Manager, to contribute to the supervision of people who have a tendency to wander, neglect themselves or put themselves at risk.

- In consultation with the Home Care Manager, remind people to take medication, if necessary.

- To be aware of the appropriate action to take in an emergency.

- After appropriate training, to comply with Manual Handling legislation when moving clients.

- To have an appropriate knowledge of the correct use of aids and equipment used by or with people in their normal daily living, and to report any obvious defects.

- To work with a client's partner or carer to maintain the client in the home.

- To provide general support to the client as part of a caring team.

- To undergo such training as is necessary to carry out the duties of a home care assistant.

Appendix 5

EXAMPLE OF A PERSON SPECIFICATION

Job title: Home care assistant

Section: Home Care

Refers to job description: Home care assistant

Physique and health

Essential

Neat and tidy appearance

Good general health record

Physically fit

Desirable

Weight for size

Attainments (general education, job training, job experience)

Essential

Good command of English

Average numeracy

Average literacy

Desirable

Caring in a personal or professional capacity

General intelligence (level and type of reasoning ability required)

Able to understand and follow instructions and policies

Able to use initiative (dealing with emergencies)

Organisational skills (able to plan workload)

Common sense

Able to undertake and benefit from training

Special aptitudes

Essential

Communication: articulate and able to report changes

Able to work as part of a team

Desirable

Speak other languages

Interests (which might be met in the job)

Housekeeping skills

Interest in people

Disposition

Flexible

Dependable

Stable

Self-reliant (able to work on own initiative)

Sense of humour

Stress tolerance

Circumstances (which might help or hinder)

Essential

Access to phone

Desirable

Own phone

Own transport

Flexible regarding availability

Other relevant factors

Appendix 6

SAMPLE INTERVIEW QUESTIONS: HOME CARE ASSISTANT

1 Pleasantries to relax atmosphere.

2 Can you tell me what you know about the home care service?

3 What particularly interested you in applying to us?

4 Have you had any experience (personal or professional) in caring for people?

5 Imagine that you are a home care assistant. How would you cope with:

Incontinence   People from ethnic minorities
Dishonesty   Confusion
Aggressive client

(Any of these can be used – make up scenarios)

6 Do you have any views on working with people who are HIV positive or have AIDS?

7 Working in home care can be stressful at times; how do you cope with stress?

8 Have you ever had to deal with an emergency?

9 Health questions:

a Home care assistants help clients to move; do you have any concerns about your back or have a history of back problems?

b You need to be physically fit; how do you rate your general health?

c How much sick leave have you taken this year? (Or last year?)

10 We provide a flexible service to clients, seven days a week, 365 days a year; what hours would you be available to work? (Discuss the need to be flexible/punctual/reliable.)

11 Do you have the use of a car for work?

12 Do you provide any foster care/respite care or assisted lodgings to clients of the Social Services?

13 Have you any questions you would like to ask us?

14 How much notice do you have to give and when would you be able to start work?

15 Have you any holiday booked?

Finally, thank them for coming and advise them when you expect to let them know the outcome of the interview.

Appendix 7

EXAMPLE OF CONDITIONS OF SERVICE

References

Advise applicants that, before offers can be made, two references must be obtained, one of which must be from the previous/latest employer.

Medical

Advise that appointments are made subject to medical clearance. Advise of the questionnaire and process and implications.

Rate of pay

Basic   Monday to Friday 6 am to 8 pm

Evenings from 8 pm

Saturday

Sunday

Bank Holidays

Method of pay

Four-weekly into a bank/building society

Termination of employment

Four weeks' notice required

Probationary period

Reviewed at three and six months; can be extended if thought appropriate

Casual staff

No annual leave or sick pay

Permanent staff – annual leave

24 days (pro rata according to days/hours per week worked), with an additional five days after five years' service.

Permanent staff – sickness

Paid from day one

Travel expenses

Car allowance: paid according to cc of car.

Insurance: advise of the clause required – 'For use by the policy holder in connection with her/his business.'

Licence: advise that this must be seen

Training

Induction: advise as to procedure – first three days not paid until six months' satisfactory service has been completed.

All training is compulsory, not optional – explain.

Protective clothing

Must be worn at all times, according to regulations.

Appendix 8

EXAMPLE OF A DISCIPLINARY PROCEDURE

There are different levels of the disciplinary procedure, which are fully explained in the Disciplinary, Grievance and Capability Guide. Depending on the offence committed, it is possible to invoke the disciplinary procedure at any stage; for example:

- Not following procedure – best dealt with through supervision.
- Serious breach of confidentiality – may require a hearing by the home care manager. The home care organiser would present. Probable outcome: oral or written warning.
- Theft – hearing by the group manager; the home care manager would present. Probable outcome: dismissal.

If a home care organiser is to present a disciplinary case to the home care manger, it should follow this basic format:

- The home care organiser will investigate the problem, interview witnesses and obtain statements etc.
- The home care organiser will interview the home care assistant and record it.
- Personnel will then issue appropriate documents and arrange the hearing. The home care assistant may be accompanied by a person of their choice, including a union representative.
- The home care organiser will present facts, any documents to prove the case, etc. At this stage the home care assistant may question any issues raised. This will take place with the personnel adviser present.

- The home care assistant presents their case as they see it. At this stage the home care organiser may question the home care assistant.
- The home care manager may question either party.
- The home care manager will then decide on appropriate action. This may be either an oral or a written warning; can find in the home care assistant's favour.
- If the hearing reveals serious misconduct, this must be referred to the Group Manager.
- Serious misconduct with dismissal as a possible outcome must be presented by the Home Care Manager to a Group Manager (senior officer). Only the Group Manager has the authority to dismiss.
- All activities in the disciplinary procedure must be supported by the Personnel Department.

Appendix 9

EXAMPLE OF ASSESSMENT OF NEED FORM

Name of assessor (print)

Date of assessment

NAME OF CLIENT

Name

Tel no

A/C no

Likes to be known as

DoB

Age

Address

Referred by

Reason

NEXT OF KIN/SIGNIFICANT OTHER DETAILS

Name

Address

Tel no

Relationship

NEXT OF KIN/SIGNIFICANT OTHER DETAILS

Name

Address

Tel no

Relationship

ACCOUNT TO BE SENT TO:

Name

Address

Tel no

A/C no

PROFESSIONAL CONTACTS

GP

Tel no

Social worker

Tel no

District nurse

Tel no

Other

Tel no

Other

Tel no

ENVIRONMENT

Housing

Access

Facilities

Others living in accommodation

Emergency access

SOCIAL HISTORY

Occupation

Family

Pets

Hobbies

Religion

RELEVANT HEALTH HISTORY

Past history

Current symptoms

Medication

Allergies

PROBLEMS ASSOCIATED WITH ACTIVITIES OF DAILY LIVING
(see Client ADL Assessment Form)

Mobility

Personal care

Toilet habits

Eating/drinking

Sensory functions

Communication

Behaviour

Mental ability

Other homecare provision

Provider

Times/days

Duties

Contact name

Tel no

Other homecare provision

Provider

Times/days

Duties

Contact name

Tel no

CARE TO BE PROVIDED BY (name of home care organisation)

Summary

Signed (Assessor)

Date

Have you completed a client ADL assessment form? If not, please do so.

CLIENT ADL ASSESSMENT FORM

(Activities of Daily Living)

Name

Address

Assessment date

Assessor

1 MOBILITY

1.1 Walking (answer by placing tick in appropriate box)

	Yes	No
1 *Walks independently and is steady*	☐	☐
2 *Walks independently but is unsteady*	☐	☐
3 *Walks with a walking aid (specify in comments section)*	☐	☐
4 *Walks with help from one person*	☐	☐
5 *Walks with help from two people*	☐	☐
6 *Unable to walk*	☐	☐

Comments

1.2 Transfers (answer by placing tick in appropriate box)

	Yes	No
1 *Can stand unaided*	☐	☐
2 *Moves from bed to chair unassisted*	☐	☐
3 *Can sit up in bed from prone position unassisted*	☐	☐
4 *Requires assistance with any of the above (specify in comments section)*	☐	☐

Comments

144

1.3 Stairs (answer by placing tick in appropriate box)

	Yes	No
1 *Can use stairs independently*	☐	☐
2 *Can use stairs with help (specify in comments section)*	☐	☐
3 *Unable to use stairs*	☐	☐

Comments

2 PERSONAL CARE

Key: **A** Can complete without help or supervision **B** Requires supervision
C Requires help **D** Cannot complete

2.1 Washing (answer by placing tick in appropriate box)

	A	B	C	D
1 *Full strip wash*	☐	☐	☐	☐
2 *Wash face and hands*	☐	☐	☐	☐
3 *Can get into and out of bath*	☐	☐	☐	☐
4 *Can wash self when in bath*	☐	☐	☐	☐
5 *Hair combing and brushing*	☐	☐	☐	☐
6 *Hair washing*	☐	☐	☐	☐
7 *Oral hygiene*	☐	☐	☐	☐
8 *Shaving*	☐	☐	☐	☐

Comments

2.2 Clothing/dressing (answer by placing tick in appropriate box)

	A	B	C	D
1 *Can select own clothes*	☐	☐	☐	☐
2 *Can make appropriate choice of clothes*	☐	☐	☐	☐
3 *Dressing*	☐	☐	☐	☐

Comments

3 TOILET HABITS

3.1 Use of toilet (answer by placing tick in appropriate box)

	A	B	C	D
1 *Daytime use of toilet*	☐	☐	☐	☐
2 *Night-time use of toilet*	☐	☐	☐	☐

Comments

3.2 Continence (answer by placing tick in appropriate box)

	Yes	No
1 *Fully continent*	☐	☐
2 *Occasional incontinence of urine*	☐	☐
3 *Frequent incontinence of urine*	☐	☐
4 *Has bladder sensation*	☐	☐
5 *Occasional incontinence of faeces*	☐	☐
6 *Frequent incontinence of faeces*	☐	☐
7 *Has bowel control*	☐	☐

Comments

4 EATING AND DRINKING

4.1 Eating (answer by placing tick in appropriate box)

	Yes	No
1 *Requires assistance with preparing and clearing meals*	☐	☐
2 *Eats with help (specify in comments section)*	☐	☐
3 *Requires full assistance with feeding*	☐	☐

Comments

4.2 Drinking (answer by placing tick in appropriate box)

		Yes	No
1	*Can prepare and drink fluids unaided*	☐	☐
2	*Needs supervision with preparing and drinking fluids*	☐	☐
3	*Requires assistance with preparation of drinks*	☐	☐
4	*Requires assistance in drinking fluids*	☐	☐
5	*Is reluctant to take adequate fluids*	☐	☐

Comments

4.3 Diet (answer by placing tick in appropriate box)

		Yes	No
1	*Eats a normal diet*	☐	☐
2	*Requires a special diet (specify in comments section)*	☐	☐

Comments

5 SENSORY FUNCTIONS

5.1 Definition (answer by placing tick in appropriate box)

		Yes	No
1	*Has own teeth*	☐	☐
2	*Wears dentures (specify in comments section)*	☐	☐
3	*Any attention required to teeth/dentures (specify in comments section)*	☐	☐

Comments

5.2 Eyesight (answer by placing tick in appropriate box)

		Yes	No
1	*Has good vision without glasses/contact lenses*	☐	☐
2	*Has good vision with glasses/contact lenses*	☐	☐
3	*Attention required regarding glasses/contact lenses (specify in comments section)*	☐	☐

	Yes	No
4 *Is partially sighted*	☐	☐
5 *Is blind*	☐	☐

Comments

```


```

5.3 Hearing (answer by placing tick in appropriate box)

	Yes	No
1 *Has good hearing without aid*	☐	☐
2 *Has good hearing with aid*	☐	☐
3 *Has poor hearing (specify in comments section)*	☐	☐
4 *Is profoundly deaf (specify communication aids in comments section)*	☐	☐

Comments

```


```

6   COMMUNICATION

6.1 Comprehension (answer by placing tick in appropriate box)

	Yes	No
1 *Understands what other people say (verbal)*	☐	☐
2 *Understands by gestures (non-verbal)*	☐	☐
3 *Unable to understand standard forms of communication*	☐	☐

Comments

```


```

6.2 Expression (answer by placing tick in appropriate box)

	Yes	No
1 *Can make themselves understood using language*	☐	☐
2 *Can make themselves understood using gestures/aids*	☐	☐
3 *Able to make themselves be understood at all*	☐	☐

Comments

```


```

6.3 Conversation (answer by placing tick in appropriate box)

	Yes	No
1 *Makes eye contact*	☐	☐
2 *Starts conversation easily*	☐	☐
3 *Uses non-verbal communication easily*	☐	☐
4 *Able to make any conversation easily*	☐	☐

Comments

7   BEHAVIOUR

7.1 Wandering/restlessness (answer by placing tick in appropriate box)

	Yes	No
1 *Purposeful movements*	☐	☐
2 *Occasional restlessness*	☐	☐
3 *Frequent restlessness*	☐	☐
4 *Occasional wandering*	☐	☐
5 *Frequent wandering; is at risk to themselves (specify in comments section)*	☐	☐

Comments

7.2 Sleep and rest (answer by placing tick in appropriate box)

	Yes	No
1 *Sleeps well at night without medication*	☐	☐
2 *Sleeps well at night with medication (specify in comments section)*	☐	☐
3 *Does not sleep well at night*	☐	☐
4 *Occasionally sleeps during the day*	☐	☐
5 *Frequently sleeps during the day*	☐	☐
6 *Always feels tired*	☐	☐

Comments

8 MENTAL ABILITY

8.1 Orientation (answer by placing tick in appropriate box)

	Yes	No
1 *Fully orientated in time and space*	☐	☐
2 *Occasional confusion*	☐	☐
3 *Frequent confusion*	☐	☐
4 *Very confused all the time*	☐	☐

Comments

Signed (Assessor)   Date:

Have you completed a client assessment form with all the client's details? If not, please do so.

Now please insert your summary of ADL onto page 2 of the client assessment form.

CLIENT RISK ASSESSMENT

NAME OF CLIENT

[ ]

ASSESSOR   **Date**

[ ]   [ ]

Complete only Part A (this form) if the answer to Question 1 is Yes (if No, complete this form, Part A, and also Part B).

PART A MANUAL HANDLING

1 Does the client need assistance with lifting or transferring? If YES complete the following questions; if NO go to part B

YES/NO

2 What assistance does the client require? Describe the lifting and handling assistance required

[ ]

[ ]

3 What is the frequency?

[ ]

4 How heavy is the client?

[ ]

5 How much is the client able to do for themselves in the act of lifting or transferring?

[ ]

6 What are the facilities in the home in the areas where lifting or transferring will take place?

[ ]

7 What assistance is in the home? (handles, aids, appliances, member of the family)

[ ]

8 Are there alternatives to any acts of lifting or transferring? (eg using a commode chair instead of wheelchair)

9 How complicated are the lifts?

10 Level of risk on a scale of 1–10.

11 Has this level of risk been explained to the client and member of staff?

12 What contingency arrangements are there if the client's condition changes or in an emergency (eg falling on the floor)?

13 What are the competency requirements and training needs for staff?

14 Who is responsible for this client and the staff?

CLIENT RISK ASSESSMENT FORM

PART B COSHH (CONTROL OF SUBSTANCES HAZARDOUS TO HEALTH)

1 Must any substances be used that are liable to be hazardous to health? If yes, specify substances:

2 Can these be substituted to reduce risk? If so, by what?

3 Has a COSHH assessment been carried out in the actual circumstances of use?

4 What advice/training needs to be given to staff handling hazards? Is this documented in the Care Plan?

5 What are the arrangements for assessment review?

6 Who is responsible?

CONTROL OF HAZARDS IN THE ACTUAL CIRCUMSTANCES OF USE

Substance

Assessor

Date:

Action required as a result of the assessment

Safe working practices written

Author

Title of the document

Date written

Dates of review

Dates of revision

First aid measures

Fire-fighting measures

Accidental release measures

Handling and storage

Exposure controls and personal protection

Design of engineering equipment

Maintenance of engineering equipment

Personal protective equipment required

Appendix 10

EXAMPLE OF CARE PLAN

REQUEST FOR PROVISION OF HOME CARE/DATA INPUT FORM

Date of request

Straightforward/Complex (delete as necessary)

Referred by

Allocated to

Surname

Address

First name

Title

Gender

Tel no

Ethnicity

DoB

Relationship of next of kin

Lives alone?   Yes/No

Next of kin tel no

Next of kin

GP name

Address

GP tel no

Service: short, medium or long term –
please comment

Keyholder

Service	Details of service required	Days	Preferred time
Personal care			
Laundry			
Meals/Snacks			
Shopping			
Housework			
Other (eg social care, sitting)			

BENEFITS PAID TO CLIENT (please circle)

Housing Benefit	Yes/No	Income Support	Yes/No
Attendance Allowance	Yes/No	Council Tax relief	Yes/No
Disabled Living Allowance	Yes/No		
Payment rate	Max/Min/NA		

DEPENDENCY SCALE (ELDERLY) (please circle)

0 1 2 3 4	Walking	0 1 2 3 4	Dressing/Undressing
0 1 2 3 4	Bathing	0 1 2 3 4	Feeding
0 1 2 3 4	WC/commode	0 1 2 3 4	Continence
0 1 2 3 4	Motivation	0 1 2 3 4	Orientation
0 1 2 3 4	Memory	0 1 2 3 4	Communication
0 1 2 3 4	Light housework	0 1 2 3 4	Heavy housework

Client type	Eligibility	Priority

	Monday		Tuesday		Wednesday		Thursday		Friday	
	Hour	Visits	Hour	Visits	Hour	Visits	Hour	Visits	Hour	Visits
Morning										
Lunch										
Tea										
Evening										

	Saturday		Sunday	
	Hour	Visits	Hour	Visits
Morning				
Lunch				
Tea				
Evening				

HELP RECEIVED/CENSUS DATA (please circle)

Meals on Wheels	Yes/No	Very sheltered housing	Yes/No
Lunch club	Yes/No	Other warden	Yes/No
CSDP	Yes/No	Crossroads	Yes/No
Daycare social services	Yes/No	Day care health	Yes/No
Short stay social services	Yes/No	Short stay health	Yes/No
District nurse	Yes/No	Relatives	Yes/No
Volunteers	Yes/No	Social worker	Yes/No
Community psychiatric nurse	Yes/No	Physiotherapist	Yes/No
Private help	Yes/No	Neighbours	Yes/No
Sheltered housing	Yes/No	Friends	Yes/No

HOME CARE ASSISTANT ALLOCATED

Tasks (normally completed by Supervisor)

Household

Personal care

Rehabilitation

Social care

Date service to start:

Date review due:

Supervisor:

Self-perceived needs and wishes

Self-care

Health

Informal network and support

Service network

Personal history

Interests and hobbies

Transport and access

Accommodation

[ ]

Finances

[ ]

Needs of carers

[ ]

Risks

[ ]

SUMMARY OF NEEDS, ELIGIBILITY/PRIORITY, OBJECTIVES TO BE ACHIEVED

Needs

[ ]

Eligibility

[ ]

Priority

[ ]

Overall aim

[ ]

Objectives

[ ]

Signed:

Consumer

[ ]

Date

[ ]

Carer

[ ]

Assessor

[ ]

Further Reading

CareFully: A guide for home care assistants by Lesley Bell, published by Age Concern see p 164)

Caring for People: Community care in the next decade and beyond, published by HMSO, London

Community Care: Agenda for action – a report to the Secretary of State for Social Services by Sir Roy Griffiths, published by HMSO, London

Community Care Handbook: The new system explained by Barbara Meredith, published by Age Concern (see p 164)

A Framework for the Development of Standards for the Provision of Domiciliary Care (£2), produced by Joint Advisory Group of Domiciliary Care Associations, and available from the Social Care Association (see p 162)

Guidance on Contracting for Domiciliary and Day Care Services, produced by AMA/ACC/ADSS (£10), and available from the AMA and the LGMB (see pp 161, 162)

Home Care – The business of caring by Lesley Bell and Linda How, published by Age Concern (see p 164)

Laing's Review of Private Healthcare (£120), published by Laing & Buisson Ltd, London

Social Trends (1995) published by HMSO, London

Standards for the Registration for Domiciliary Care (£5), produced by the Joint Advisory Group of Domiciliary Care, and available from the Social Care Association (see p 162)

Professional press

Community Care

Care Weekly

Homecare Professional

Training material

OPAL 2 Open and Assisted Learning for Managers of Care Services, UNISON Education and Training

Integrated Care Awards, NVQ 2 and 3, Care Sector Consortium, Local Government Management Board

Crediting Competence Workbook of Management Standards, Management Charter Initiative

Health and Social Services Management (six modules), NHS Training Department

Useful Addresses

Age Concern England
see p 163

Association of County Councils
Eaton House
66A Eaton Square
London SW1W 9BH

Tel: 0171-235 1200

Association of Independent Care Home Advisers
58 Southwick Street
Southwick
Brighton
East Sussex BN42 4TJ

Tel: 01483 578160

Association of Metropolitan Authorities (AMA)
35 Great Smith Street
London SW1P 3BJ

Tel: 0171-222 8100

British Association of Domiciliary Care Officers (BADCO)
c/o Kate Telfer
46 Wolverhampton Road
Stafford ST17 4DS

Tel: 01785 58167

Care Sector Consortium
(Occupational Standards Council for Health and Social Care)
3 Devonshire Street
London W1N 2BA

Tel: 0171-436 8712

Carers National Association
20–25 Glasshouse Road
London EC1A 4JS

Tel: 0171-490 8818

Counsel and Care for the Elderly
Twyman House
16 Bonny Street
London NW1 9OG

Tel: 0171-485 1566

Department of Health
Richmond House
79 Whitehall
London SW1A 2NS

Tel: 0171-210 3000

Publications Department
DoH Store
Health Publications Unit
No 2 Site
Manchester Road
Heywood
Lancs O40 2PZ

Elderly Accommodation Council
46A Chiswick High Road
London W4 1SZ
Tel: 0181-995 8320

Help the Aged
16–18 St James' Walk
London EC1R 0BE
Tel: 0171-253 0253

Joint Advisory Group of Domiciliary Care Associations
see Joint Initiative for Community Care

Joint Initiative for Community Care Ltd (JICC)
6 Minerva Gardens
Wavendon Gate
Milton Keynes
Bucks MK7 7SR
Tel: 01908 585373
Fax: 01908 582064

Local Government Anti-Poverty Unit
35 Great Smith Street
London SW1P 3BJ
Tel: 0171-227 2878/2812

Local Government Management Board
Arndale House
Arndale Centre
Luton LU1 2TS
Tel: 01582 451166

Management Charter Initiative
Russell Square House
10–12 Russell Square
London WC1B 5BZ
Tel: 0171-872 9000

National Council for Vocational Qualifications
222 Euston Road
London NW1 2BZ
Tel: 0171-387 9898

NHS Training Department
St Bartholomew's Court
18 Christmas Street
Bristol BS1 5BT

Office of the Data Protection Registrar
Wycliffe House
Water Lane
Wilmslow
Cheshire SK9 5AF
Tel: 01625 535777

Social Care Association
23A Victoria Road
Surbiton
Surrey KT6 4JZ
Tel: 0181-390 6831

UNISON Education and Training
20 Grand Depot Road
London SE18 6SF
Tel: 0181-854 2244
Fax: 0181-854 0708

United Kingdom Home Care Association (UKHCA)
42 Banstead Road
Carshalton Beeches
Surrey SM5 3NW
Tel: 0181-288 1551
Fax: 0181-228 1550

About Age Concern

Managing CareFully is one of a wide range of publications produced by Age Concern England, the National Council on Ageing. Age Concern England is actively engaged in training, information provision, fundraising and campaigning for retired people and those who work with them, and also in the provision of products and services such as insurance for older people.

A network of over 1,400 local Age Concern groups, with the support of around 250,000 volunteers, aims to improve the quality of life for older people and develop services appropriate to local needs and resources. These include advice and information, day care, visiting services, transport schemes, clubs, and specialist facilities for older people who are physically and mentally frail.

Age Concern England is a registered charity dependent on public support for the continuation and development of its work.

Age Concern England
1268 London Road
London SW16 4ER

Tel: 0181-679 8000

Age Concern Cymru
4th Floor
1 Cathedral Road
Cardiff CF1 9SD

Tel: 01222 371566

Age Concern Scotland
113 Rose Street
Edinburgh EH2 3DT

Tel: 0131-220 3345

Age Concern Northern Ireland
3 Lower Crescent
Belfast BT7 1NR

Tel: 01232 245729

Publications from ◆C◆ Books

A wide range of titles is published by Age Concern England under the ACE Books imprint.

Professional handbook series

CareFully: A handbook for home care assistants
Lesley Bell

This highly acclaimed and accessible guide provides practical advice on the day-to-day tasks home care assistants encounter and addresses issues such as legal responsibilities and emotional involvement.

£9.95   0-86242-129-2

Home Care: The business of caring
Lesley Bell and Linda How

Tackles, head on, the problems faced by anyone wishing to set up a new home care business or already running one. Using a question and answer format, advice is offered and key issues are highlighted. The text includes key aspects of the Community Care Act; getting started; contracting; business planning and cash flow; and managing the business.

£14.99   0-86242-212-4
To be published May 1996

The Community Care Handbook: The reformed system explained
Barbara Meredith

Written by one of the country's leading experts, the new edition of this hugely successful handbook provides a comprehensive overview of the first two years of implementation of the community care reforms and examines how the system has evolved. This second edition is essential reading for all those keen to keep up to date and fully informed on the ever-changing community care picture.

£12.95   0-86242-171-3

Business Skills for Care Management: A guide to costing, contracting and negotiating

Penny Mares

Negotiating contracts can be a time-consuming and complicated business for seasoned professionals. It can become a minefield to those with little direct experience in the area. Always practical and accessible, this easy-to-understand book for care managers guides the reader through all the key stages involved, always emphasising that the aim is to achieve the best quality service for users.

£9.95   0-86242-191-8

To be published Summer 1996

Expanding Care: A practical guide to diversification for care homes

Jenyth Worsley

This handbook outlines some of the ways in which care homes can diversify their activities – including the provision of domiciliary, day and respite care. It offers advice on assessing local needs, marketing and tendering, and explores the practical arrangements surrounding implementation.

£14.95   0-86242-154-3

Cooking for Elderly People

Alan Steward

An important resource for anyone responsible for providing food for older people, this manual is packed with advice and guidance. It contains extensive information on what is good nutrition as well as 120 tried and tested ideas and recipes.

Co-published with Winslow Press

£17.50   0-86388-067-3

If you would like to order any of these titles, please write to the Mail Order Unit, Age Concern England, PO Box 9, London SW16 4EX, enclosing a cheque or money order for the appropriate amount made payable to Age Concern England. Credit card orders may be made on 0181-679 8000.

Information factsheets

Age Concern England produces over 30 factsheets on a variety of subjects, which are revised and updated throughout the year. Single copies are available free on receipt of a 9″ × 6″ sae. For information about charges for multiple copies and about the annual subscription service, or to order factsheets, write to the Information and Policy Department, Age Concern England, 1268 London Road, London SW16 4ER.

Index

accidents: insuring against *31–33*; reporting *30–31, 54, 124–127*

accreditation *34, 80–81, 83, 85*

advertising: of services *34–36*; for staff *47, 57, 60, 61*

aims, setting *21, 38, 39*

APEL *106*

application forms *61*

'approved providers' *35, 80–81, 85*

assaults (on staff) *54*

assessments: of client needs *12, 13, 14, 15, 17, 90–91, 138–149*; of risks *see* risk; of staff *68, 69, 70, 71*

BACS *29*

banks *22, 26, 29, 30, 36*

bathing, help with *8, 16*

bequests, policy on accepting *46–47*

business plans *20–26*; s*ee also* financial aspects

care managers *16*

care plans *13, 16, 95–96*; reviewing *96, 98*; sample *154–158*

caseloads, deciding on *57–58*

charges *10, 18*

cleaning services *8, 12*

co-ordinating care *95, 97*

Community Care Plans *13, 25*

community care policies *12–15*

complaints procedures *31, 43–44, 97–98*

compliments procedure *31, 98*

computer software *27, 29, 72*

confidentiality *45–46, 49*

contracting for services *13, 76–77, 83–86*; *see also* contracts

contracts *77*; block *16, 26, 30, 78–79*; cost and volume *79*; individual service *79–80, 94, 96*; monitoring *87*; negotiating *86–87*; spot (price by case) *16, 26, 78*

costs *18*; unit *27–28*

death: and counselling *72*

debts, payment of *29*

demographic changes *11, 14*

disciplinary procedures *73–74, 136–137*

discrimination *40, 48, 94, 95*

emergency procedures *54–55*

employment conditions *48, 49, 134–135*

equal opportunities *47, 48, 60*

ethnic communities *50, 58, 94*

financial aspects: charges *10, 18*; management of *23, 26, 27–30*; *see also* insurance; money, handling

gifts, policy on *46, 47*

grievances, dealing with *74*

handbooks, provision of *66*

harassment of female staff *58, 94–95*

health and safety *17, 64, 72, 51–55, 91–92*; *see also* risk assessments

home care *7–8*; changes *10–12*; and community care policies *12–15*; providers *15*; purchasers *16–18*

home care staff *see* staff

immunisation *53, 72*

independent sector *12, 13, 15, 17–18, 21, 28, 29, 76, 95*

infectious diseases *53, 72*

information, sending out *60–61, 63*

insurance *31–33, 48*

interviews *47, 48, 62, 63*; exit *74*; sample questions *132–133*

job descriptions *48–49, 59, 128–129*

keys, marking 45

leaflets, information 34–35, 44
legacies, policy on 46–47
legislation 33–34, 51–54
lifting 51, 52, 53
local authorities: and community care 13–15, 16, 25, 76–77; 'in-house' service 15, 16, 17, 28
Local Government Management Board diplomas 105, 106

managers 37–38, 69–71, 89–90; assessing own competence 107–112; identifying strengths 99–101, 105; see also under NVQ
marketing services 34–36
medication, administering 8, 16, 53
meetings, staff 50, 70, 71, 72
money, handling 46–7

needs, assessing see assessments
NHS trusts 13, 16, 17, 76
nursing care 8, 16, 33, 49, 58
NVQ awards and standards: care 40, 42, 48, 50, 51, 59, 67; management 68–69, 105–106, 114–117

objectives, setting 21, 38, 39
'on-call' systems 73
OPAL 2 package see UNISON
overheads 27, 28

pensions, collecting 46
private sector see independent sector
probationary periods 64
proformas 22
publicity material 34–36

quality assurance 41, 43, 44, 45, 89

records, keeping 30, 31, 46, 97
recruitment of staff 47–48, 56–63
references, obtaining 61, 62
registration 18, 34, 80–82, 85
residential homes 11, 14, 15, 18, 28
'rights' (of clients) 40, 54
risk assessments 17, 52, 54, 91–92; and confidentiality 45; sample forms 118–123, 150–3; see also accidents
rotas, staff 72–73

safety see accidents; health and safety; risk assessments
service specification 76, 83, 85, 87
shift work, patterns of 73
shopping, procedures for 46
shortlisting candidates 62
social services see local authorities
Special Transitional Grant 13, 14, 76
staff: defining requirements 57–58, 59–60, 130–131; matching with clients 58–59, 94–95; recruiting 47–48, 60–63; supervising 37–38, 69–71; see also training
standards, setting 41–42, 43
supervision of staff 37–38, 69–71

targets, setting 21, 39, 42
tendering 76, 77, 85
time, effective use of 101–103
time-recording systems 71
training 48, 49, 50–51, 53, 64–69; in investigating complaints 44; management 105–106; see also NVQ
travelling expenses 49

UNISON (OPAL 2) 36, 51, 65, 90, 106

values, underpinning 39–41, 103–104
VAT 18, 34
visiting clients (by managers) 92–94
voluntary sector see independent sector